WORKING TWICE AS HARD

THE REALITY OF ENTREPRENEURSHIP FOR BLACK WOMEN

QUINISHA JACKSON-WRIGHT

Subjects: Non-fiction, Race, Entrepreneurship, Black Women, Self-Help, Women in Business

Paperback ISBN: 978-0-578-86116-6

Ebook ISBN: 978-0-578-86118-0

To the Black women working twice as hard

CONTENTS

Introduction   vii

1. Sweet dream...or a nonprofit nightmare   1
2. The leap (or push?) from a 9-to-5   14
3. Healing from work wounds   26
4. The cost to be a boss   37
5. I just want to be successful   46
6. Same shit, different (work) day   57
7. Putting on a brave face   67
8. Back in bed with the enemy   80
9. Does a golden ticket exist?   89

Acknowledgments   99
Notes   101
About the Author   105

INTRODUCTION

In 2019 I had a chat with another Black woman, whom I'll call Rhonda, about being the only Black person in a mostly white workplace. We spoke about how isolating it is when no one looks like you, along with the pressure of feeling like you have to represent an entire race. Rhonda added though, an upside to a "seat at the table" as the only Black person. For her, a seat at the table offers an inside look at what "they" are talking about, and gives leverage to underrepresented folks in the room. Her stance echoed what I told myself while I spent over a decade trying to get a seat at the table. Through fierce determination (and a little bit of luck), I eventually obtained the coveted seat. Once I finally got to that seat, I expected something magical to happen. Surely, I thought, the others at the table would be awed by the blood, sweat, and tears it took for me to be there.

They'd recognize my brilliance, talent, and tireless work ethic, and quickly implement the ideas I had to make improvements, which would pave the way for others like me to get to the table. Imagine my disappointment, when that magic ceased to ever materialize. Instead, the white people at the table smiled and greeted me warmly, but never acknowledged the fact there was no one around who looked like me. They asked for my input on how to be more inclusive, only to continue with the same practices. When I shared ideas, they spoke over me, interrupted me, or ignored me completely. Eventually they stopped asking for my input altogether.

This made me question why I was so focused on being at the table in the first place. After years of denied opportunities and barriers set in front of Black folks long before I existed, what made me think anything would change once I finally got in? How did I know if I was even getting a true inside perspective on what "they" were talking about? After all, wouldn't it be easy to withhold information because "they" knew I felt indebted just to be there?

These questions raced through my mind daily, leading to mental and physical exhaustion. I wondered if I was really brilliant or talented. Maybe my work ethic wasn't as great as I thought? The only rewards for my contributions were microaggressions and more tasks added to the workload. Is this what I worked so hard to be a part of? After years of working to get into the "exclusive" spaces that rarely make room for people like me, reality sank in:

They didn't want me there.

When I say they didn't want "me," I mean me as an individual. They certainly wanted a person of color to be there, specifically a Black woman, to mark off another box on their diversity checklist. They were happy to have me while I displayed mannerisms that made them comfortable.

But they didn't want me there if I asked too many questions. Or if I raised my voice. Or if I refrained from small talk because my mind was distracted by news of another Black body being shot down. They didn't want all of the parts that make me "me."

So I left the table.

My physical and mental wellbeing is a bigger priority than trying to fit the standards of whiteness. Plus, I believe Black people are brilliant enough, talented enough, and creative enough, to build our own table. We don't have to claw our way to a spot at tables full of hatred and bias toward us being there. Our value is too great to be limited by the spaces still unconcerned with whether we succeed or fail.

I understand some Black folks still want a seat at the table. Rejecting the table is a scary move to make, and one that holds an unknown amount of risk. I'd rather take a chance and build a table for others like me, than fight to be at one where I'm not welcome.

I wrote these words days after I traded my job for entrepreneurship in April 2019. Before I quit, I tried to ignore the microaggressions, office politics, and subtle racism at work, for the sake of a steady income. The problem though, was that I became a shell of myself with each day of increasing toxicity. Instead of feeling confident about my skills, I fretted over every project as an outcome of my boss's ego-fueled criticism.

Five months into the job, I learned I had high blood pressure during a routine doctor's visit and was immediately put on medication—at the age of 32. This jarring wake-up call proved the "ignore red flags" tactic was a serious threat to my health. *Do I want to be miserable for years to meet my career goals?* I asked myself. *Am I willing to emotionally—and even physically—die for a paycheck?*

If you've read this far, you know the answer to that. While playing the game at a 9-to-5 seems like the best bet, working for yourself can actually be less risky when you're a Black woman. For years, I thought working for someone else was my only option to make a living. Once I discovered the world of entrepreneurship, it opened my mind to a different approach that fit my personality and lifestyle goals.

Working Twice as Hard serves as a guide for Black women on the path of entrepreneurship, or who don't know where to start. I won't lie: Being an entrepreneur is hard. Being Black is hard. And being a woman is hard. When you're all three, your chances of success move farther and farther out of reach, contrary to what our "pull yourself up by the bootstraps" culture tells you. This book offers insight on how to make strategic moves to sustain yourself as an entrepreneur.

Each chapter breaks down a specific aspect of entrepreneurship and how it impacts Black women, including mental health, finance, and running a business in the digital age. You'll read my personal anecdotes as an entrepreneur, along with stories from other Black women. I share data to back up our stories (for all my fellow research nerds!), followed by practical tips to help you avoid the mistakes I made. As the future of the workplace shifts due to events like the COVID-19 pandemic, business savvy provides an extra layer of protection in an unstable economy. Whether you choose to work a traditional job and build a business on the side, or pursue self-employment full-time, entrepreneurial skills are crucial to stay competitive in the rapidly changing climate.

Most of all, I wrote this book to validate Black women going through what I did. As I progress through my career, I realize how harshly I've been treated, simply for being a Black woman. Every day we show up at jobs that tell us we're too loud, too opinionated, too bossy, too assertive. But it's not us. It's the toxic work culture that gaslights us and tries to keep us quiet at every turn. I'll speak for the Black women who don't have the words to describe their own experience. My hope is for us as Black women to shift our focus from the 9-to-5 grind, to building our own legacies.

ONE

SWEET DREAM...OR A NONPROFIT NIGHTMARE

My journey into entrepreneurship began after a dream job turned out not to be so dreamy. After five years in the military, I completed my bachelor's degree and was on the hunt for my first "real" job. I worked several jobs before my military days, most of them low-paid retail and customer service gigs. They paid the bills, but hardly came close to the glamorous career where I could rock a power suit and heels like I daydreamed about as a kid.

I was convinced my degree would open the door to that career, plus a higher salary. During my final semester of undergrad studies in spring 2018, I eagerly sent out my resume for roles in the communications field. I got a call two weeks after graduation from the HR manager at a nonprofit in Southern California where I'd applied for a position. I was living in St. Louis, so I went through an initial phone interview, then a video interview with the management team.

There were delays in between each stage of the interview process, which I chalked up to normal office operations. I was asked to complete an assessment that included writing a sample press release, making edits to an internal document, and giving suggestions to improve an existing marketing campaign. Although I've been writing most of my life, I had never done so in past jobs and it felt good to put my skills to use professionally.

I waited anxiously to hear back after turning in the assessment. From what I'd been told previously, the next step would be an in-person interview with the organization's senior leadership. To my surprise, I received a call a few weeks later from the HR manager with an official offer. They were impressed with my writing skills and wanted me to start as soon as possible. Accepting the offer was a no-brainer for me.

The role was in my field, located in a town right off the Pacific coast, and came with a $60,000 per year salary. Until then, the most money I'd made at any job was around $40,000 annually. Excited for the opportunity, my then-husband and I quickly made arrangements to sell our belongings and relocate from St. Louis in July 2018. Once we found housing and got settled, I started in August and shifted my focus to being successful in my new role. I received a warm welcome from my team, complete with lunch at an upscale beachfront restaurant that first week to celebrate my arrival. The job offered a flexible schedule and I could choose to work from 8-to-4, 9-to-5, or 10-to-6. I woke up each day to get to the office promptly at 8:00 am.

Within the first two months, I volunteered to put together the agenda for my department's weekly meetings and assist my supervisor with the internal communications update. I finished all of my assignments prior to anticipated deadlines, assisted other staff members with projects, learned how to use Adobe InDesign, and took advantage of several professional development opportunities.

From dream job to nightmare

Despite this, the atmosphere of the nonprofit started to make me doubt whether this role was the right fit for me. For one, I was the only Black woman. From the first day I stepped into the office, I was hyper vigilant of everything from my physical appearance to my mannerisms. I didn't realize it at the time, but this was behavior influenced by what's called "stereotype threat."[1] The term, coined by psychologists Claude Steele and Joshua Aronson, refers to the perceived opportunity of confirming a negative stereotype related to one's identity such as race or gender. For me, this meant avoiding any gestures that would categorize me as an "angry Black woman." In the past, strangers and friends alike told me I looked mean, so I made sure to turn on the charm at my new job. I smiled, laughed politely at my colleagues' jokes, and mimicked their body language to present myself as friendly and approachable. Although no one explicitly made note of me being the only Black woman at work, the dynamic alone made me feel I had to prove I belonged there.

My boss, an openly gay Black man whom I'll call Tim, seemed like someone I could rely on in the predominantly white workspace. He was active in the local LGBTQ+ and social justice spaces, both of which I wanted to get involved in. During my first couple weeks on the job, he offered to introduce me to other Black folks in the community. I had high hopes for a positive work relationship, but reality quickly set in. While Tim was publicly friendly to me, his nonverbal cues made it clear we weren't equals. At work events, he was more likely to schmooze with powerful philanthropists than make conversation with junior employees. The introductions he promised early on never came about. He was in and out of meetings throughout the work week or locked away in his office.

Aside from our weekly one-on-one sessions, it was rare to have a face-to-face conversation with Tim unless he was tasking me with a last-minute assignment to complete before the end of the workday. The best way to describe his behavior most of the time was transactional. He used language that made it sound like he was in my corner—i.e., "you're a rockstar" and "we're a team"—but it came across as inauthentic. The lack of a genuine connection left me feeling like a warm body at a desk, similar to my time in the military. In boot camp, it was common for trainers to refer to a new personnel member as a "body" or "recruit." For women, we also had the honor of being addressed as "female." I thought the days of being treated less than human were behind me, but I was clearly mistaken.

I began to sense a power struggle between Tim and myself. Before I started, he was responsible for composing internal communications emails for staff. I offered to take on the task so he could focus on other projects. The emails normally went out every other Friday and I put together an update while he was out of the office one week. I sent a draft to his direct supervisor —I'll call her Shannon—to make sure everything looked good, and she gave me the go-ahead to send it to the rest of the staff.

Upon his return, Tim pulled me aside and chastised me about a line item in the email on upcoming job openings the HR manager requested to include. When I mentioned that I got approval from Shannon, he said she wasn't privy to "HR stuff" and it would be best to wait for him to approve emails in the future.

Another time, Shannon mentioned that she wanted the communications team to attend meetings with other nonprofits in town and learn about their work. She told us to take a look at her calendar and reach out if there were any organizations we'd like to know more about. I asked her if I could tag along for a meeting with a local organization that focused on women's entrepreneurship. She enthusiastically agreed and after the meeting, she shared with the rest of our team how impressed she was that I took the initiative.

Again, Tim pulled me aside to say I should have told him I went to a meeting with Shannon. As my supervisor, he insisted I loop him in so he could introduce me to different organizers. Since he was always busy, I honestly didn't want to bother him and it seemed odd to get this kind of feedback in light of Shannon's reaction. I cared about the nonprofit's mission and wanted to make a good impression, but Tim's criticism left me feeling like I did something wrong. That, plus his demands that I constantly give him updates, clashed with my independent work style.

Exchanges like this, along with passive-aggressive emails and Slack messages, came out of the blue from Tim and increased from every other week to almost daily occurrences. Other than "good morning" exchanges and office break room small talk, I had little interaction with my co-workers. Being new in town, I hoped to develop some friendships, especially with the other women, but they seemed to have no interest in connecting outside of work hours. I shared creative marketing and communication ideas, which Tim dismissed, while he added busywork without advance notice. I considered voicing my concerns to the HR manager, who I had a fairly pleasant relationship with. But due to cautionary tales from friends and family, along with my own work history, I decided against it. The cardinal rule for workplace conflicts in my experience usually came down to this: "HR is not your friend."

These jobs ain't loyal

My first eye-opening encounter of how unfriendly HR folks can be came courtesy of an experience while living in Atlanta. After I spent almost a year looking for work, my roommate helped me get hired in his department at a trucking company in the summer of 2009. I came on as a part-time employee, but made enough money to live comfortably, a relief after months of being behind on credit card and student loan payments. The job was going well—until I made a mistake and was fired a few months later in February 2010.

It all started when I was randomly selected to take a drug test. I worked a regular shift in the billing department from 6:00 pm to 12:30 am, but I was tasked with going to the clinic at 9:00 am the next day. I dragged myself out of bed to complete the test, only to find the clinic closed that morning. I called the clinic several times to figure out what was going on, but no one answered. I went to work later that day and told my supervisor what happened, who gasped in horror. As a newbie at the job, I didn't realize it was a big no-no to miss taking the drug test before I started my shift.

After my supervisor's discovery, I went through a series of events that involved writing statements and explaining what happened to the HR manager. I was suspended the next day and would have to wait to find out if I still had a job pending investigation. I fought back tears until I got to my car, then sobbed uncontrollably on the drive home. The suspension happened on a Thursday, and I spent the whole weekend stressing over what the outcome would be. Monday rolled around and I still hadn't heard from anyone, so I called my supervisor for an update. She reluctantly broke the news that they decided to terminate employment due to my "refusal" to take the drug test.

I was so wound up over what happened, I didn't sleep for days after. This abrupt and sobering incident revealed a new truth to me about work culture: No one cares about qualifications or your dedication to a job. There are procedures to adhere to, and if you step outside of them, a job holds the power to end your livelihood in a matter of days—or less. Before I got fired, I was one of the most accurate billers in the department. I was always on time and got along well with my co-workers. None of that mattered once I violated the company's zero tolerance drug-testing policy. That humiliating experience made me reluctant to lean on HR for support at future jobs, because I now understood they'd look out for the best interests of the company first and foremost.

The breaking point

With that in mind, I struggled to figure out my next move at the nonprofit job. I'd worked there for less than a year and feared my short time in this role would be a turnoff to other potential employers. Plus, I doubted another job was the true answer to my problems. The issues at the new job mirrored the same ones I came across in the past, including my time in the military. At each job, I knew the vibe was going south when anxiety gripped my chest at the start of the workday, as I wondered what bullshit I would inevitably have to face.

In March 2019, six months into my first "real" job, I felt the same anxiety grip my chest as I approached the office each morning. I was in therapy and said positive affirmations to start my day. While getting ready for work, I looked in the bathroom mirror and repeated to my reflection, "I love myself. I have a purpose. My life has value."

All of that did nothing to alleviate my constant anticipation of what microaggression awaited me moments after getting to my desk. I felt lost, disappointed, and mentally and emotionally drained. If both military life and civilian employment weren't for me, what else was there? I finally saw a light at the end of the tunnel—working for myself. I frequently scrolled through the #beyourownboss and #entrepreneurlife hashtags on social media, but never thought it was anything I could make a reality. As I started to question my dream job, I signed up for a coaching session with a freelance writer to get help with bringing in more work. After the coaching session, I ramped up content on my blog to establish myself as an authority in the personal finance space. My plan was to wait until I hit the one-year mark, then make the switch to self-employment. Only my boss's behavior got worse, and I jumped —or felt pushed—to leave four months earlier than I planned.

Communication with Tim continued to erode. In March 2019, I asked to attend a conference that took place the same week as an annual work event later that year. While the work function was only one day, the conference which focused on content for finance bloggers, was a week-long event. Everyone at my job knew I blogged about finance and encouraged me to learn more about the industry. I even got Tim's approval to attend a weekend retreat on women's personal finance in February. I wasn't sure of the protocol for the upcoming conference and emailed Tim to ask if arrangements could be made to avoid schedule conflicts.

After he ignored my initial email, I sent a follow-up message. Tim said we could discuss it in our next one-on-one meeting. When we met, he declined to give me a direct answer and said it was my decision to go to the conference. If I missed the work event, he added, I wouldn't be considered a team player. I asked if this would overshadow other contributions I made to the team since I started. He changed the subject. I was disappointed with his decision to give an ultimatum rather than show true leadership and work out a reasonable compromise. I later suggested a compromise of my own, where I would attend the work function and take the rest of the week off for the conference. Tim said it was an "excellent compromise," then informed me I had to write a short essay on why I wanted to attend the conference. I agreed, although I eventually resigned before both events.

On a separate occasion, Tim dumped a box of quarterly reports onto my desk with no verbal communication while doing so. Weeks later, he sent a message via Slack with a reminder that quarterly reports were to be filed away in the office storage space. This was an item on the "quarterly report to-do list," which he drafted up on a whim about a month earlier. While filing quarterly reports wasn't the problem, his act of dropping them at my desk without a word made me feel like a lowly peasant ordered to launder a sack of soiled rags. Or a child whose parent silently slips a list of chores onto their lap with only a brief moment of eye contact that says, "You know what to do." The gesture was a display of Tim's increased determination to assert his dominance. Being a dominant and headstrong person myself, this move triggered me and I took it as an insult to my intelligence.

I was still frustrated by his lack of support about the confer- ence, especially the comment that I wasn't a team player. My husband and I moved thousands of miles across the country, to an expensive town full of white people, just for this role. My first week on the job, at Tim's request, I rented an F-150 truck— a vehicle I had never driven before—to transport chairs to a work event an hour away. I routinely overlooked racially insen- sitive comments from co-workers and donors who clearly never had a conversation with a Black woman in real life. Like the time at a fundraiser when an older white woman asked if I hated my first name as a child. How the hell was I not a team player? All of my frustration over the previous six months came to a boiling point, and I refused to stay quiet anymore.

I briskly walked into his office and asked why he sent a Slack message instead of speaking to me directly about storing the reports. He said he assumed I knew what to do with them since it was on the to-do list. My voice trembling with anger, I told him not to drop items on my desk again without saying what he wanted. The veteran in me wanted to include several choice words to emphasize my point, but I restrained myself and went back to my desk. Moments later, Tim suggested we go for a walk, where he mentioned he had felt tension between us for several weeks.

He briefly discussed some better ways for me to communicate, then said my approach was unprofessional and would be noted in an upcoming performance review. My heart sank. Despite my careful moves to avoid backlash for being an angry Black woman, it was happening already. I could barely concentrate on my work the rest of the day. My mind was consumed with the humiliation of having a negative remark on my first performance review. The hours dragged until it was time to go home, where I spent the night drowning my sorrows in a bottle of wine.

TO MAKE MATTERS WORSE, my personal life wasn't much better. Only two years into marriage, my husband and I were barely out of the honeymoon phase before we had to deal with the headaches of unexpected financial setbacks, drama with in-laws, and rowdy neighbors. When I got the job offer in California, we saw it as a fresh start not only career-wise, but for our relationship. That fresh start soon fizzled out, as the beauty of the West Coast proved to be no match for our marital woes. Shortly after I started the dream job, we were back to our regular arguments about everything including money, household chores, and alone time—as an introvert, I needed it more than he did. Sometimes the arguments lasted until the early hours of the morning. I'd get a few fitful hours of sleep before going into work to deal with the office hostility. To say I was overwhelmed puts it mildly.

After the box dumping incident, I noticed signs that Tim was building a paper trail around our interactions. If he mentioned a low-priority item in passing and I neglected to complete it within the same day, I'd get an email from him that this was an example of my lack of communication to improve

on. At the end of some emails, he'd offer to sit down with me
and the HR manager for further discussion. My faith that he
genuinely cared to work out our differences was at an all-time
low, so I never took him up on the offer. By April, my anxiety
would spike every time his name popped up in my inbox or
whenever he passed my desk. It felt like my every move was
under a microscope. I braced myself for the possibility of a
write-up or worse, another termination. My anxiety progressed
into regular moments of breaking down in tears in the office
bathroom. Silent tears, as I was careful not to draw attention
from co-workers passing by. I thought some time away might
be what I needed, so I took a week of vacation. The day I
returned from vacation, Tim made a snide comment in our
department meeting because I paraphrased an item on the
agenda he dictated to me in an earlier email, instead of writing
it verbatim.

"I wanted to discuss another priority item...which isn't on
here for some reason," he said with raised eyebrows and an
exaggerated eye roll. My co-worker, a white man, didn't notice
the slight or pretended not to notice, and looked on silently. I
pointed out that the item was included, but not word-for-word.
Tim waved his hand dismissively and claimed it wasn't a big
deal. *Why all the drama then?* I wondered, though saying it out
loud would probably lead to another chat about my profes-
sionalism.

Instead, I gave my two-week notice that afternoon, four
months ahead of my one-year work anniversary in August. The
same day, HR broke the news to my colleagues via email, which
said I was moving on to pursue new opportunities and wished
me the best. When I spoke to co-workers who asked where I
was off to next, I smiled and said I would be freelancing. No
one on my immediate team acknowledged my departure, aside
from a couple brief sentences in a farewell card.

The trade-offs of entrepreneurship

Once I moved into entrepreneurship, I realized I wasn't alone in making the decision to be my own boss. According to the American Express 2019 State of Women-Owned Businesses Report, Black women represented the highest rate of growth in starting a business compared to any other demographic, both between 2014 and 2019, and between 2018 and 2019.[2] Further, we made up 21 percent of all women-owned businesses, the largest segment after white women. Since the release of the American Express report, numerous articles highlight how many Black women are starting our own businesses and applaud how brave we are for stepping out on our own. Yet a somber aspect of this statistic is rarely addressed. Like me, many Black women decide to work for themselves because it's the lesser of two evils—the other evil being a soul-draining, dead-end career. We've grown tired of toxic work environments, daily microaggressions, and racism. Rather than wait to be laid off or fired on a technicality, we take matters into our own hands to avoid further humiliation.

Entrepreneurship though, comes with another series of hurdles and harsh trade-offs. Because we leave our jobs as a means of survival, we often do so without the financial resources to keep us afloat as we build our own businesses. While we eliminate the stress of mental abuse in the workplace, we trade it for the stress of trying to expedite our business's growth to replace the salaries we gave up. The savings we build to give ourselves a cushion evaporate within months, while client leads continue to trickle in slowly, if at all. Sometimes we land a new client, only for the contract to fall through weeks or months later. This is all while making the adjustment from employee to employer, and still dealing with the trauma of years in unhealthy workplaces.

For those who have yet to make the transition, I don't want

to discourage you from being your own boss. Entrepreneurship can be a beautiful experience and has mentally and emotionally liberated me in many ways. My goal is to bring balance to the idea that entrepreneurship is the golden ticket for Black women. Similar to the American dream that promises a good job, home, and nice car if you work hard enough, entrepreneurship can leave us disheartened if we don't go into it with our eyes open.

TWO
THE LEAP (OR PUSH?) FROM A 9-TO-5

The allure of entrepreneurship is hard to resist, even for the most dedicated 9-to-5-er. While a stable job usually means you've made it in life, self-employment is the trendy career move in the digital age. Being your own boss is often glorified. Mainstream media depicts self-employed life as sleeping in whenever you want and working in your PJs, instead of long commutes and sitting in a cubicle for eight hours a day. Motivational quotes like "Live like most people won't, to live like most people can't" flash across the newsfeeds of almost every social media platform.

The remote lifestyle of a digital nomad looks even more tantalizing. Who wouldn't want the freedom to work from anywhere? As the colorful #digitalnomad Instagram captions and photos will display, "anywhere" can range from the lush countryside of Europe, to tropical landscapes in South America. When you're in a dimly lit office with your eyes glazing over from staring at the same Excel spreadsheet for hours on end, you wonder why you haven't already put in your two-week notice and started your own entrepreneurial venture. *If everyone else is doing it, why can't I?* You think. *It can't be that hard, right?*

I've learned the freedom of self-employment comes with a price. Within nine months of moving 2,000 miles to California, I was on the rocky freelance path that started a chain of life-changing events, including the decision to end my marriage. Just two months after I resigned from my job, we filed for divorce and I was left alone to heal from my career and relationship troubles. Here's what the leap looked like for me, along with eye-opening facts about Black women at work. And to help you avoid some of the mistakes I made, I'll share four tips on how to prepare for a potential career jump.

Life at work for the Black woman

If you're a Black woman, the idea of being your own boss is especially appealing. As Black women, we have a history of troubles navigating the traditional workplace. In the piece titled "Racism and Sexism Combine to Shortchange Working Black Women," Jocelyn Frye describes how Black women's issues in the labor force date back to slavery, when we "faced sexual violence and exploitation to produce free labor without rights" to our own children.[1]

Even after the abolishment of slavery, Black women's work options were limited to low-paying domestic service roles, such as cooking, cleaning, and caregiving for white families. As of 2019, Black women make up a third of those employed in service jobs, compared to one-fifth of white women.[2] It doesn't get easier for those of us who obtain advanced degrees and land the often-coveted office jobs. Research shows that women of color are more frequently assigned "office housework," such as taking notes for meetings or ordering lunch for the team.[3] Being assigned these duties makes us less likely to be promoted than our white or male counterparts, as we have fewer opportunities to display our skills in more valuable ways. However, should we refuse to perform housework tasks, we face the risk of being penalized.[4]

Other microaggressions against Black women in the workplace include being spoken over in meetings, harsher criticism for mistakes,[5] and bias against our natural hair.[6] In 2019, California passed the CROWN Act, a law that protects Black women against discrimination at work and school based on our natural hair.[7] While this technically appears to be a win, the win feels bittersweet. After all, if you talk to any Black woman, she'll tell you about the intolerance of Black women's hair for decades—maybe even centuries. The protection that we *might* get with these new laws seems minor compared to the years of mistreatment we've endured for the hair that grows from our scalps. It also goes along with society's inclination to ignore Black women's issues until they're deemed legally valid.

And if we're not being discriminated against because of our hair, we still have to prepare for inappropriate comments about it from co-workers, usually intended as compliments. I've been riddled with anxiety seconds before walking into work with a new hairstyle. A million thoughts would race through my mind:

Who will say they like my hair?

Who will claim they didn't recognize me because of my new 'do?

Which co-worker will try to stroke my tresses as if I'm the latest American Girl collectible doll?

How do I avoid said co-worker?

IT SOUNDS SILLY, but it happened every time I went into the office with freshly installed box braids at my nonprofit job. Most of my co-workers exclaimed, "Love your hair!" and went on their way, with the exception of one white woman, a senior executive. She'd stop at my desk, stare in amazement, then whisper excitedly, "I wish *my* hair could do that!"

I was never sure what she meant by "that," but feared the conversation would get more awkward if I dared to ask. Plus, as a junior employee, I anticipated backlash from senior management if I voiced my discomfort. Instead I chuckled politely, attempted to send telepathic signals for her not to touch me, and breathed a sigh of relief when she walked away. Though they seem harmless, these reactions to Black women's hair add to the tension that comes with being the only person of color at your job. This dynamic puts the onus on Black women to actively avoid unwelcome comments, or take on the task of educating others whenever we decide to switch up our hairstyles.

As annoying as the hair issue is, it pales in comparison to other obstacles Black women face when we're underrepresented at work. Because many professional environments are predominantly white, Black women find ourselves being the "only," and deal with external and internal pressure to represent all Black women to disprove negative stereotypes. In addition to the professional challenges Black women navigate, we're up against greater financial barriers. While women overall earn less than men, Black women make between 61 to 67 cents for every dollar earned by our white male counterparts. This translates to more than a $946,000 deficit in lifetime earnings, based on a 40-year career span.[8]

Even when we ask for a raise, women of color are 19 percent less likely to receive one than white men.[9] Earning less money for the same work, while dealing with subtle and overt acts of racism and sexism, leaves Black women feeling isolated, burned out, and stuck in our respective careers. It leads you to wonder if the alternative of entrepreneurship is truly a choice, rather than a desperate attempt to escape the impossible standards of a traditional work environment.

Work PTSD is real

When you hear about post-traumatic stress disorder (PTSD), it's often limited to conversation around challenges it causes for military veterans after war combat. As the expectations of the traditional workplace intensify, some of us find ourselves with similar PTSD symptoms and emotional scars from previous jobs.

I know what you're thinking. *PTSD from an office job? Are you serious right now?* It's hard to imagine how much trauma can result when you have your own desk and free office snacks. The nature of the cushy office job is commonly a cover-up for toxic behavior. At a job where your day consists of meetings and follow-up emails, you tell yourself you have no room to complain when someone makes a weird comment about your hair. When you make more money than you ever have, you dismiss the passive-aggressive behavior from your co-workers during daily interactions. Like when you're washing your Tupperware in the break room kitchen sink and they reach across you to empty their coffee mug without saying, "Excuse me." After your boss leaves you out of the loop on an important project, you convince yourself it was an accident.

You might not realize it, but the stress of a quietly hostile environment changes you. The confidence you once had in your work, is now tainted with self-doubt. Before you know it, you're afraid to share your opinion in meetings. Or if you have the courage to share, you instinctively brace yourself for the "Well, actually…" responses from your team. Over time, each morning you walk into the office, you feel as if you're going to war. Only this war comes with insincere smiles and business casual attire instead of camouflage and combat boots. If this sounds familiar, you're not alone. Based on results from the Everest College 2013 Work Stress Survey, 83 percent of participants reported stress from at least one aspect of their jobs.[10]

Among these reasons were low pay, poor work-life balance, and lack of opportunity for advancement. Further, job stress in the United States is estimated to result in more than $190 billion in healthcare costs and 120,000 deaths per year.[11] With these numbers, it's startling that our culture treats job stress as a minor inconvenience rather than the life-threatening hazard it is.

As bad as job stress is for all employees, the dangers are magnified for Black women. In the essay "The Psychic Stress of Being the Only Black Woman at Work," Maura Cheeks describes the unique challenges that come with being Black and female in the corporate world.[12] "In the office, we're not really supposed to think about race, unless it's part of our job description," she writes. "But for [B]lack women, that's almost impossible."

She continues, "Being [B]lack and female at work means navigating insensitivities with dignity and assuming that most people are not ill-intentioned." This resonates with me, as I thought, *They didn't **really** mean that*, whenever I found myself on the receiving end of a "harmless" comment about my name or hair in a professional setting. Though these comments have no place in a work environment, I've been in the world long enough to know any reaction besides a polite smile and forced laugh, would swiftly place me in the "Angry Black Woman" category. Once you're in that category, you could win the Nobel Peace Prize and still not live it down.

Like in the first chapter, when Tim said I was unprofessional after I spoke up about him dumping work on my desk. Until then, I never raised my voice or pushed back on requests from anyone on my team. Yet instantly, after a brief moment that involved no profanity, physical aggression, or property damage, I faced punishment in the form of a negative mark on my personnel record. While the language to describe my reaction was based on supposed standards of professional conduct, the underlying message was clear: "Don't challenge authority. Don't speak up for yourself. Don't question me...or else." When this is the outcome of being transparent at work, it's difficult—if not impossible—to keep your mental and emotional wellbeing intact. You've heard about my experience. Now here's a story from a Black woman who chose entrepreneurship to support her family and mental health needs.

A shift in priorities

For Kassandra, founder of BridgeTech Enterprises, self-employment was part of a strategy to prioritize her mental health. She shared in a phone interview that she worked for herself on and off since 2012.[13] Kassandra pursued entrepreneurship a few years later and started her own engineering project management consulting firm.

"I didn't say I was going to start a business right away. I had enough experience as a project manager—and in life—where I could potentially make that transition. I wanted to restore order to my mind and I knew it had to happen regardless of going to another job or if I started my own thing."

As a Trinidadian immigrant who lived in Canada most of her life before moving to the states, she needed flexibility to care for her mother, who lived in Montreal and has since passed away.

"I was a long-distance caregiver and traveled a lot to Canada to look after my mother's wellbeing. It wasn't a question of a want but a need in terms of my lifestyle," she told me.

With more freedom and a healthier work-life balance, Kassandra doesn't regret the decision to be her own boss. Still, she's aware of the challenges that come with entrepreneurship as a Black woman, especially the financial variance.

"We're at a huge disadvantage in terms of funding," she

shared. "We typically have to pull from our own personal funds...if we even have them."

She's noticed disparities in the support Black women receive when starting a business, compared to Black men. When a Black man chooses self-employment, Kassandra says, the decision is framed positively by family and friends. Meanwhile, a Black woman's loved ones might suggest she's "not ready" for such a big challenge.

"It seems that when a Black woman takes the risk to move into self-employment, there's a different conversation," she said. "You get a lot of questions like, 'Are you sure it's a good idea?'"

A 2014 study with a sample of 85 Black men entrepreneurs and 58 Black women entrepreneurs found indicators that women trailed men in firm performance, task-specific efficacy, and opportunity recognition.[14] Whether this is due to a lack of underlying community support, remains a question. Data is limited on Black entrepreneurs in general, and there's less information on differences in success between Black women and men entrepreneurs. Kassandra's family and friends offered plenty of support after she left her job. That support, plus a financial safety net, gave her time to heal and figure out her next move. She recommends other Black women prepare financially before they leap into self-employment. "Save three months of expenses or whatever feels comfortable, to keep yourself afloat at the start of a new business venture," she said.

While this is valuable advice, you might run into obstacles as you build an "FU money" fund, as it's known in the personal finance community. If you're not familiar with the term, this is the amount of money you should set aside to be comfortable with flipping the bird to your job when you've had enough. Like the good personal finance writer I am, I had nowhere near three months of living expenses saved when I quit my job. It made sense to stay employed until I had a healthy savings cushion, but stress from the office was getting worse each day. I worried no amount of savings could undo the damage if I stayed much longer. If you want to try out self-employment, but don't have enough money saved to feel comfortable taking the leap, I get it. Quitting your job isn't for everyone, and it's not a decision to be made lightly. That said, I've worked enough soul-sucking jobs to know that staying put for a paycheck, only lasts so long. Here are some tips to help if you're ready to make the switch.

Ramp up savings

Setting aside money for unexpected life events is something you should always do, even if you have no intention of leaving your job. If you think it's time to move on, accelerating your savings will help you get ready.

If you've been aggressively paying off debt, consider making minimum payments instead. That way you can bulk up the cash cushion for the "how to quit your job" fund. The same goes with putting away money for retirement, which I wish I had done in hindsight. At my previous job, I only needed to contribute four percent of my paycheck to get a 100 percent employer match, but I increased my contributions to six percent.

Once I knew I was going to resign, it would have helped to decrease the contributions to four percent and put the extra money into an easily accessible savings account. Now I have a lump sum of retirement savings, but I can't touch it any time soon without incurring hefty penalties. You live and learn though. Life is full of twists and turns, so don't think you're a failure if you slow down on debt repayment. It's temporary and having cash on hand to float you during a career transition, will help relieve some stress.

I'd also caution you not to lock yourself into a set amount of money to save before you quit. Once you hit your target savings goal, you'll probably ask yourself if even that much is enough. I'm not telling you to quit with $3 in your bank account, but consider other factors aside from the cold hard numbers. Can you mentally and emotionally handle staying at your job for another six months to a year while you save? Is it possible to reduce your hours or work remotely so you can focus on your next move? Would you be able to find a part-time job to bring in some income until you earn a full-time salary from your business?

I was drained when I got home from work and had little energy to pitch new freelance clients. Once I quit, it gave me the clarity to market and build a steady client roster. Everyone's tolerance for a stressful job is different. Staying might *seem* like the better option, but you'd be surprised what you can accomplish when you leave a toxic 9-to-5.

Rethink the way you handle expenses

Your biggest concern is probably how to cover bills once you quit your job. One way to alleviate this is paying ahead on as many bills as possible. If you can, instead of paying monthly on expenses like renters and car insurance, pay the one-year or six-month premium upfront. You'll have the coverage you need, and one bill off your plate, for the next several months. This also helps give you peace of mind if your first couple months of business are shaky. Life as an entrepreneur is unpredictable and I've learned never to anticipate money until I have a signed contract or partial deposit—or both.

Another strategy to give your future self some relief, is to stock up on a few months' worth of toiletries. Think: Toilet paper, soap, toothpaste, body wash. If you have these products, plus non-perishable food items on hand to last you during a lean business period, this frees up cash flow for bigger expenses like rent, utilities, and insurance. If you have credit card debt, contact your credit card company and ask to lower your interest rate. I learned this hack a few years ago and negotiated a lower rate on two credit cards. It doesn't seem like much, but every little bit helps when you're planning a career change.

Network with like-minded people

When the news got out that I was resigning from my job, my co-workers' responses ranged from "Congratulations!" to "Oh my gosh, is everything okay?" This did nothing to slow down the rollercoaster of emotions I was on. During my switch to self-employment, I connected with friends who took the leap from traditional jobs. I'm grateful for amazing people like Kristin Wong, Melanie Lockert, and Jackie Lam, who are killing it in the freelance game. They've shared practical tips to help me do the same and offered much-needed support.

If you don't have like-minded people in your immediate circle, you can find them at local meetups, professional conferences, and co-working spaces. To find an online community, try LinkedIn, Twitter, and online forums like Reddit. Virtual workshops and webinars are also good places to connect. It might feel awkward to approach strangers online or in person, but don't be shy! Keep it casual when you introduce yourself, share a little about what you do, and that you'd love to know more about their work. A word of caution: You don't want to be the person who only reaches out when you need work. Make it a habit to bring value to the entrepreneur community. Share helpful information you come across, refer clients who might be a fit, and generally be a nice human being. This networking style pays off more than hustling on your own, trust me.

Take time off before you jump into entrepreneur mode (seriously)

Leaving a job to work for yourself, even under amicable conditions, is a loss. We usually think of loss when a loved one passes away, but you're likely to feel the same wave of emotions with a major career change. You're giving up the comfort of a steady paycheck, and the comfort of fitting in with people who still work traditional jobs. The next time someone asks, "What do you do?" you can't rattle off a fancy title with an easily recognizable company. When many of us tie our identities to jobs, the impact is heavier than you think.

Give yourself time to acknowledge this after you leave your job. I applied the advice "Never leave a job without another one lined up" when I started freelancing full-time. The week after I left my job, I was sending out cold emails, while onboarding two new clients. Looking back, I wish I gave myself a week or two to reflect, rather than jump into hustle mode.

Don't do what I did. Take some time out for yourself. Journal, meditate, go for long walks, or whatever helps you unwind. Some days, you might stare into space and daydream for a while. That's perfectly fine. Whether your move into entrepreneurship is a leap or a push, you'll need a clear mind to prepare for all the surprises that come with it.

THREE
HEALING FROM WORK WOUNDS

During my five years in the U.S. Navy, bureaucracy and office politics reared their ugly heads on a daily basis. Although I mostly kept to myself, I developed a reputation at my command as "the one with an attitude" and was subsequently blackballed by senior leadership. This meant I routinely received "must promote" evaluations instead of "early promote" evaluations, making it less likely for me to be promoted in rank. Despite the subpar evaluations, I obtained all required job qualifications and had no misconduct on my record. I got no support when I expressed interest in switching from my job as an electrician to a paralegal. In fact, my desired career change prompted snarky comments from the department head that I was "going behind his back" when I did on-the-job training with the paralegal staff after working hours.

Any time the department needed to send someone on a temporary work assignment, my name was at the top of the list. As a result, I spent years doing work that had nothing to do with my job. 2015, my last year in the military, was especially hellish. A new crew was on board that enforced even stricter rules, especially for those with an "attitude." As an E-4, I was tasked with jobs normally reserved for an E-1, like cleaning storage spaces and cargo handling. For non-military folks, this would be like assigning a corporate employee with five years of experience to make daily coffee runs. I heard rumors that management was plotting to get me kicked out with an other-than-honorable discharge. This is the military equivalent of a felony conviction, and if it happened, I'd lose access to my benefits as a veteran, including education assistance, VA home loan eligibility, and health care. It would be arduous to find a job with that mark on my record.

I was required to join my command for a second deployment although I only had months left in my contract, and my requests to use earned time off were denied. Being deployed on an aircraft carrier with limited communication with friends and family, I felt isolated. There were days when I fantasized about jumping off the ship into the open sea, just to get away from it all.

Instead, I started seeing the ship therapist. I shared fears about making the transition back to civilian life, and my resentment toward the department leaders. This didn't magically resolve my issues, but it helped me hold on until the day I flew back stateside. In March 2016, I received my discharge paperwork and felt the weight immediately lift from my shoulders. My exit from the Navy was the first of many steps I'd take to heal from the emotional scars of the workplace.

The fight against failure

The same feelings of depression and isolation crept up again at my nonprofit job. While I wasn't confined to a ship, no one at the office felt safe to confide in. My therapist and husband offered as much support as they could, but work stress consumed me. When I got home, I'd rant for hours about the bullshit that happened each day, then go to bed and wake up to do it all over again. And unlike the military, there was no end date to count down to. I refused to go back to the low point from my deployment days, even if it meant letting go of an opportunity I wanted badly a year before.

After I left that job, I naively thought my emotional and mental stress would disappear. Little did I know, it was only beginning. It didn't help that my marriage ended two months after I resigned. I knew for a while we weren't on the same page, but was afraid to say it out loud. Much like leaving my job after nine months, I expected judgment from friends and family once they learned we divorced within three years. Several months of working through my fear of judgment in therapy helped me accept that if I wanted peace, I had to take a leap of faith in my personal and professional life. Accepting the truth though, didn't make either choice easy. Weeks after my last day at work, and again after the divorce paperwork was signed and my husband moved out, I questioned whether I made the right decision. When I left the military, I dreamed of a successful career and marriage, and failed at both in record time. *What's wrong with me?* I thought. *Am I having an early mid-life crisis?*

But there was no time to seek out answers to those questions, or so I told myself. Without a spouse or steady paycheck, I was in a sink-or-swim scenario, and I promised myself I wouldn't sink. Determined to prove that my divorce and brief nonprofit employment didn't make me a failure, I jumped headfirst into building my business. Even when I cried for hours at night over the back-to-back losses, I pushed through the following day and sent out pitches to bring in work. I was mentally exhausted most days, but continued to network online and in person for freelance prospects. Around the same time my husband and I split in summer 2019, I started a part-time remote job to supplement freelance income. I smiled and small talked my way through virtual meetings, when all I wanted to do was stay in bed. I resigned from that position a few months later, once I admitted—to myself and my therapist—I was still devastated from the loss of my nonprofit job.

Letting go of the remote gig pushed me back into full-time entrepreneurship in fall 2019, where I adhered to the structure of past jobs. I woke up each morning around 7:00 am and promptly got to work no later than 8:00 am. I was set on working an eight-hour day, even if there weren't eight hours of work to do. Any emails or last-minute requests from clients, I tried to handle immediately. When my workday was technically done, I still checked email "just in case." Although I traded in working for someone else to be my own boss, I wasn't feeling too boss-like. I soon felt the same resentment from employment, toward my clients when they dragged their feet on deliverables or went radio silent on email correspondence. I was physically free from the 9-to-5 life, but the mental and emotional chains continued to weigh me down.

Working twice as hard

If you've decided on entrepreneurship to escape an unhealthy work situation, you're likely still dealing with the emotional aftermath of your old job. Leaving a toxic job is the same as leaving any toxic relationship. You feel relief once you're out of it, but the emotions and memories from the past, spring up when you least expect them. I saw entrepreneurship as an opportunity to prove my worth in a way I felt had been stolen from me. Part of me hoped my old bosses would hear about my accomplishments through word of mouth and be ashamed of how they treated me. The "use your haters as motivation" mindset felt energizing at first, but it came with consequences I didn't anticipate. I took on clients who weren't the best fit, for the sake of bringing in income. I'm a prompt, clear, organized, and strategic communicator. I like to be paid well and on time

—but who doesn't? I still agreed to work with clients who were disorganized, unsure of the content they wanted, slow to respond to emails, and paid woefully low rates due to their tight budget.

I jumped through hoops for clients who were more than happy to reap the benefits of my labor. After all, who wouldn't love to have a freelancer do all the work an employee would, for a flat fee instead of a salary and benefits? Meanwhile, I had the double burden of inconsistent income and stress from trying to exceed client expectations. I was quickly trapped in the same cycle of burnout and depression I experienced while employed. I occasionally talked to freelance friends about my dilemma, but didn't want them to think I was in over my head. After several encounters with clients who flaked out on projects or wanted me to do a lot of work for a little money, it was time for something different. Otherwise, I'd continue to suffer from the same wounds I did while working for someone else.

Growing up in a Black household, the unspoken rule is you have to work twice as hard as white folks to get ahead in life. I applied that rule throughout my school years, from elementary to college undergrad. Any grade below a B, felt like a knife to the heart. I never passed up an extra credit assignment, even when I was guaranteed to pass the course. If I didn't perform at the highest level at all times, I criticized myself for being a slacker. I carried this obligation into every job and was always on time, met every deadline, and eagerly took on any task, big or small.

My dedication to going above and beyond, only got me a pat on the head and more tasks added to my workload. I accepted it because I figured my time would come. Most career advice centers around proving yourself to employers, whether it's during the interview process or when you're up for a promotion. Those who sacrifice their wellbeing, families, and social lives, are praised for being team players. If you never question your organization's constantly shifting priorities, your boss graciously thanks you for being flexible. Your colleagues rave about how passionate you are if you work long hours without extra pay. I held myself to the same standards as an entrepreneur, without realizing it at first. Once I admitted I needed help, I began to unlearn some of the habits I picked up in the workplace.

I talked to my therapist about the transition to entrepreneurship. I shared feelings of guilt about whether I was working hard enough to be successful. I mentioned working from 9-to-5 when I didn't want to and being available to my clients at a moment's notice. We talked through what it would look like if I let go of those old ways since I was on a different path. By the end of 2019, I no longer forced myself to stick to a 9-to-5 schedule. I resisted the urge to immediately respond to clients' emails and pushed back when they made requests outside the original scope of work. If a client prospect couldn't afford my services, I wished them the best and parted ways. As a result, I instantly felt more in control of my time and workload. Now focused on my own needs instead of an employer's, I moved another step forward in the healing process.

Living up to expectations

When you first start working for yourself, it's normal to be afraid to say no to clients or take a step back from the everyday hustle. You're running a one-woman show after all, so there's no one else to pick up the slack. Unlike a job that comes with a built-in team, entrepreneurs have to take on the roles of marketing, accounting, legal, and admin, to name a few.

The great part about working for yourself is you don't have your boss looking over your shoulder. The same challenge is you don't have your boss looking over your shoulder. Without a conventional authority figure, you *are* the authority figure.

The problem is, instead of being the cool boss who lets us off early for the day, many of us choose to be the tyrant with a never-ending to-do list. To take care of business, we hustle 24/7 and give ourselves no time for rest.

The stakes feel a lot higher when you start your own business than the workplace. Let's say you started an entry-level position at a major corporation. No one would expect you to become the CEO of that same company within your first six months of employment. It's easy to understand it could take several years, if ever, to get to that level of your career. There's a different expectation when you own a business. If you're not making six figures within the first six months of self-employment, you might think you're a failure for not growing quickly enough. What we don't realize is the early years of entrepreneurship are the equivalent of working in an entry-level role. If you don't make six figures in the beginning, that's actually normal. The glamorization of entrepreneurship that highlights business owners who make millions in their first year, sets the standard the rest of us work desperately to meet. We're conditioned to expect immediate success, rather than allow the time it takes to build a sustainable business. A side effect is the same distress we tried to get away from as employees.

Entrepreneurship + mental health

Mental health experts are taking a closer look at the challenges of entrepreneurship, especially for Black women. Dr. Joy Harden Bradford, a licensed psychologist and host of the podcast *Therapy for Black Girls*, dedicated an episode to the topic, where she and Samara Stone, LCSW-C, spoke candidly about the obstacles entrepreneurs face.[1] One of the challenges Stone mentions, is the reality that we have to handle all the responsibilities of running a business and not just the ones we enjoy. "We want to do the work [we love] but don't think as much about other moving parts," Stone said. "It takes discipline to do the things you don't want to do. There's no supervisor that requires you to do anything, but your business will suffer if you don't take care of it."

They also discussed "decision fatigue," which many new business owners experience as we sort through the overwhelming amount of resources on entrepreneurship. Depending on where you look for advice to build your business, you'll be bombarded with marketing strategies including email lists, LinkedIn, Pinterest, Instagram, Twitter, Facebook, and direct mail. With so many possibilities, Stone says, "Instead of trying to do everything all the time, you can choose to do the things that move the needle for your business in a significant and meaningful way."

She says it's time we normalize the challenges of running a business, and dismiss the notion that asking for help makes us weak. Finally, she shares a strategy that's simple, but hard to do when you're a people pleaser—like myself.

"[I learned] to say no to things that weren't important to me. So often we allow others to set the priorities, to set the agenda for how we use our time, spend our energy, and pour out our creativity. Learning how to say no, opens the door for you to say yes to the things you want."

Powerful words indeed. Here are a few more ways to help you practice self-care during your entrepreneurship journey.

Get comfortable with saying no

When I first started turning down low-paid freelance work, my anxiety went through the roof. I had a million thoughts about the response I'd get, if I got one at all. *Will they laugh at me for thinking I deserve more money? What if I can't find any work after I turn them away?* After I said no, something amazing happened.

Life went on.

Each client prospect thanked me for my honesty, and said they'd get in touch if they had more room in their budget later on. The world didn't explode. There was no angry mob waiting at my door to persecute me. I've learned it's okay to say no, and encourage other entrepreneurs to do the same. When you work for yourself, this is more important than any skill or creativity you bring to the table. The more time and energy you put into working for peanuts, the less time you have to find higher-paying work. The less time you have to find higher-paying work, the longer you'll remain trapped in the cycle of being underpaid. Eventually you'll burn out, and you might even give up and go back to traditional employment. There's nothing wrong with working a 9-to-5, but it should only happen if you *want* to go that route. Not because you can barely stay above water with self-employment income.

If you have a hard time saying no, take baby steps. The next time a client reaches out with an unexpected request, respond with, "Let me think about it and get back to you." Or if you say yes out of habit and realize you should have declined, follow up later with, "I know I agreed to take on [insert request], but I've given it more thought and decided I won't be able to commit after all." No need to be overly apologetic or offer too much explanation because life happens and circumstances change. Your first few nos will feel awkward, but you'll figure out how to turn down requests in a way that works for your personality and business style.

Don't be afraid to ask for help

I'm stubborn. And proud. And fiercely independent. These are good traits to have as an entrepreneur, but they work against me at times. Remember how I said I was too embarrassed to talk to other freelancers about my difficult clients? That was my pride getting in the way. If I talked to them sooner, it would have saved me the headache from struggling alone.

No matter how many books you read, seminars you participate in, or coaches you work with, you won't have all the answers when you start working for yourself. And that's okay. If you get stuck at some point in your business, don't be ashamed to reach out for support. It can be as simple as posing a question in an online forum or outsourcing admin work to a virtual assistant. Like the experts discussed on *Therapy for Black Girls*, asking for help doesn't mean you're weak. It's a sign of strength and maturity to acknowledge when you need outside support and will move you closer to your business goals.

Protect your energy

As your business grows, you'll be flooded with emails, texts, and DMs from folks who want to "pick your brain." Before you even make the decision to say no, do what you can to protect who has access to you, and when.

Habits like checking emails at set times throughout the day or putting your phone on "Do not disturb" can do wonders for your mental wellbeing. I'm the type who feels obligated to respond to texts and emails as soon as I see them, so when I set these boundaries, I immediately saw improvement in my stress levels. Self-discipline is hard, so use whatever technology hacks you need to maintain peace of mind.

Plant seeds and let them grow

I'm guilty of planting seeds in my business, only to turn around and water them so much, they nearly drown. Sometimes we get caught up in the planting phase of entrepreneurship and don't allow room for natural growth to occur. If you've networked consistently for the past year, take time to nurture the relationships you've built, rather than seek out new ones. If you've built the perfect sales funnel for your product or service, give it a couple months to bring in revenue before you make tweaks here and there.

Journal about your business journey to get perspective on what you've done so far. When we're on the grind, it's easy to overlook the milestones we've reached and focus on what we have yet to accomplish. When you look back at where you were a year, month, or week ago, you'll recognize what you've reaped from the planting phase.

Growing a successful business takes a lot of patience. There's always something new you can do with your business, but you need downtime to notice how much progress you've actually made. Once you've laid the foundation, take a step back and let the universe work its magic.

FOUR
THE COST TO BE A BOSS

When I decided to leave my job, I did so with $40,000 of student loan debt, plus $3,000 of credit card debt accumulated from the cross-country relocation in 2018. I had a couple months worth of savings, a few thousand dollars set aside for retirement, and no generational wealth to fall back on. I was quite literally, going into entrepreneurship on nothing more than a hope and a prayer. I'm envious when I come across stories of—usually white women—business owners who worked at a corporate job for years and slowly built their business on the side. After growing a solid clientele along with a sturdy savings cushion, they quit their jobs and moved smoothly into entrepreneurship, sometimes landing their former employers as clients. My journey into entrepreneurship feels way more risky and somewhat foolish, compared to theirs.

Then I think about the alternative. Would I have the option to stay at the same job for five to ten years and slowly grow a business in my free time? In the piece "African Americans Face Systematic Obstacles to Getting Good Jobs," Christian E. Weller describes how Black workers' unemployment rates go up higher than their white counterparts when the economy

declines.[1] It also takes Black workers longer to find employment once the economy bounces back, in a phenomenon aptly
referred to as "last hired, first fired." Once my work relationship with Tim turned sour, it seemed naive to think I wouldn't
end up on the chopping block sooner than later. I could tough it
out until I was laid off or fired, but I went through that before
and wasn't eager to do it again. Leaving on my own terms was
better for my mental health, but came with the cost of starting
entrepreneurship on a shaky foundation.

The statistics on wealth for Black women—or lack thereof—
mirror my experience. Our ongoing battles for equal pay in the
workplace, combined with obligations like student loan debt,
play a major part in the stress of leaving a steady paycheck for
entrepreneurship. In "Debt Is Holding Black Americans
Hostage," Dr. Edna Bonhomme shares chilling statistics,
including the fact that Black women in America between the
ages of 36 and 49 have a net worth of $5, compared to the
$42,000 net worth of white women in the same age group.[2] In
addition, Black women have more outstanding student loan
debt than our white counterparts, at $29,501 in undergraduate
loans compared to $20,210 for white women. With the large
amounts of debt Black women carry, and the ever-present wage
gap that keeps us living paycheck-to-paycheck, we're vulner-
able if a 9-to-5 turns uncertain. From the start, self-employment
comes at a disadvantage without sufficient resources before
taking the leap. Here's a look at some of the costs of working
for yourself as a Black woman, followed by four strategies to
help you position yourself for financial success.

The tax of being a Black woman

America has a long history of subtly placed devices that put a
financial hardship on women and people of color. One is the
rarely spoken-of "pink tax" that women pay for clothing,

hygiene, and household products, compared to men. A 2015 study of gender pricing in New York City found that women's products cost more than men's 42 percent of the time.[3] For example, the average cost of shampoo and conditioner for women averaged $8.39, while the same product for men averaged $5.68, for a price difference of $2.71. These gendered costs start as early as childhood, with a total price difference of $14.92 between girls' and boys' toys and accessories. It's estimated that women pay at least $1,300 per year in extra costs due to the pink tax. Over 40 years, that means women are forking over an additional $52,000 for basic necessities.

Then there's the "black tax," which can be even more costly. Although the term "black tax" is most often used to describe high-income Black professionals who financially support family members, there's another tax that plagues the Black community. Black people regularly incur higher interest rates than white borrowers on everything from mortgages to car loans and credit lines.[4] A 2019 UC Berkeley study found that during the mortgage loan application process, Black and Latinx borrowers were offered interest rates at an overall mean of nine basis points (0.09 percent) higher than that of white applicants.[5] Lending discrimination practices currently cost Black and Latinx homeowners $765 million in additional interest per year. Either the black tax or the pink tax alone have negative long-term effects, but together they can be financially crushing for Black women. While undetected by the naked eye, these taxes present more obstacles that make it difficult to jump into entrepreneurship the way our white peers do.

"I'm (too?) bossy"

For Black women about their coins, sometimes the natural traits that help us earn more are repressed at an early age. As a young girl, I'd round up my cousins and give them step-by-step instructions before games like "Tag" and "Simon Says." It felt good to designate responsibilities and keep everyone organized, until one of my cousins blurted, "You're too bossy!"

My instinct was to emphatically deny it. At eight years old, I learned early there was nothing good about being bossy. I gradually stopped using my voice, for fear of hearing the B-word again. The word "bossy" haunts me until this day, along with variations like "aggressive," "mean," or my favorite, "unprofessional." These negative labels are typically attached to Black women, especially in professional settings. When we take initiative for major projects, we're controlling, while our white colleagues are deemed ambitious. When we voice our opinions about inequities, we're called bitter, while others are praised for their bravery. We're told every day to "tone it down" to avoid making men and white folks uncomfortable. But as an entrepreneur, if you're not assertive, it's going to cost you.

Why? Because being bossy translates to making money. When you run a business, you have to negotiate contracts, push back on lowball offers, or walk away if a client can't afford you. Think of women like Michelle Obama, Rihanna, and Issa Rae, who wrote best-selling books, launched multimillion-dollar empires, and landed deals with major brands. They didn't achieve all of this by sitting back quietly. Even if you don't aspire to be the next Michelle Obama, you have to be firm to get the money you deserve. Take it from me—no one else will do it for you. It's easier said than done though, when Black women deal with social pressure to "tone it down" from early childhood. This creates another layer of difficulty to position ourselves for financial success as entrepreneurs.

Now that we've covered some of the challenges that come with building income as an entrepreneur, here are a few tools you can use to get paid what you're worth. I'll be honest: These techniques aren't 100 percent foolproof. Still, they'll help you set realistic expectations for what you need to sustain yourself as an entrepreneur.

Be intentional about your rates

My first freelance client was a colleague who I reached out to about writing blog posts for her career coaching business. We negotiated pricing and eventually agreed on $50 per blog post. I thought I was balling. (Picture Scrooge McDuck swimming in dollar bills.) I worked with that client for over a year. It was around this one-year mark when the idea of freelancing full-time started poking at me. I ran some numbers to figure out how much I should charge to make my dream of full-time freelancing a reality. Then I calculated my monthly expenses and how much time it took me to complete writing projects.

It's tempting to blurt out the first number that comes to mind when a client asks your rate. Before you take that approach, consider factors aside from the actual work you'll be doing. Does the client already have a contract on hand or will you draft one? Will you need to check in with them as you complete different milestones throughout the project? What business expenses come with the project for you to do your job efficiently (i.e., client management software, shipping fees, office equipment)?

Create a list of the services you offer and potential costs of doing business. And don't forget about taxes. As self-employed folks, we're responsible for those too. Good times! Once you have solid numbers for what it takes to run your business, you'll have a better picture of how to quote your pricing. When I did this, I realized I was severely undercharging and raised my rates over time.

Another good rule of thumb is to charge clients double the hourly salary from your last job. For example, if you made $20 an hour, your minimum hourly rate would be $40 an hour.

Note: Your hourly rate is for your own knowledge and not to be shared with your clients. Remember, you're not an employee anymore. Take that hourly rate and present it as a project fee to your client. As a writer, if it takes me five hours to complete a blog post at a $40 hourly rate, I would quote a flat $200 fee. Setting rates is overwhelming at first, but it gets easier as you take on more client work and get a feel for the time and level of difficulty required.

Prepare for the costs of entrepreneurship

In my first year of self-employment, my focus was on how much money I would make. I barely gave thought to how much I'd *spend* that first year. My reality check on the costs of running a business came early. I jumped for joy when my first big client paid a final invoice. That joy turned to disappointment when I noticed PayPal deducted a processing fee from my earnings. Another wave of disappointment hit when I deducted 30 percent for taxes. Then again when I got an email reminder for my yearly web hosting service renewal. Just like that, the money dwindled to nothing and the #selfemployment life felt pretty damn bleak. Sometimes the excitement of entrepreneurship can make you overlook the not-so-fun parts—like quarterly taxes. Spending money on your business isn't glamorous, but it's less painful when you're prepared. Here are a few expenses to anticipate along the way.

- **Startup costs** — It takes money to get a business off the ground. How much money will depend on what kind of business you start and what it needs to operate. For most self-employed folks, this can include registration as an LLC, renting an office space, or buying new equipment. Like a new car or home purchase, this is the stage when your wallet gets hit the hardest. The upside is these are mostly one-time expenses. It stings at first but look at it this way: You've freed up money to spend on other areas of your business—and trust me, there are plenty.

- **Marketing materials** — I pay a yearly fee for my domain and website hosting, about $300. In today's market, a professional website is essential for any business. It helps you establish an online presence and market services or products to your target audience. Depending on what services you provide, you might pay for a logo, T-shirts, and other "swag" to garner interest in your brand. These prices vary based on your budget and desired quality.

- **Operating expenses** — You need tools to keep you organized. Technology offers a sometimes-overwhelming amount of resources to manage your daily operations. To keep track of the cash flow for your business, use accounting software like Wave, QuickBooks, or FreshBooks. These tools help you determine how much money you have coming in and out. They also come with features like invoice reminders, to cut down on time chasing clients for payment. Then there are automation tools for scheduling social media posts like Buffer or Hootsuite. You might need customer relationship management (CRM) software like Insightly, an email marketing platform like Mailchimp, or a collaboration app like Slack. Each platform comes with different price plans based on your business size and needs.

- **Miscellaneous costs** — Ahh, miscellaneous. That

fun, mysterious word for all the expenses you never think about until they pop up. For me, this is everything from PayPal processing fees, to the cost of a P.O. Box rental when I realized it wasn't a good idea to use a home address for my newsletter. Just like in your personal life, there's always an unexpected expense in business, some that you can write off on your taxes the following year. In the meantime, set aside a portion of your revenue for miscellaneous costs as a cushion for any surprises.

Reframe your business language

I cringe when I hear fellow entrepreneurs say they're going to "ask" a client for a raise. The whole point of being your own boss is to set the standard. This includes when you raise your rates, and how much. Instead of asking your clients for more money, get into the habit of telling them what you need upfront. You don't have to be an asshole, but it does require being bossy. I usually reach out to clients at the end of the year to let them know I'll be increasing my rates. I send an email that says something like this:

"Hi [name], I've enjoyed working together this year and learning more about the projects at [insert company]. I wanted to give a heads up that as of [date], my rates will increase to Y. Please let me know if you have any questions or concerns. Thanks!"

Resist the urge to give background on why your rates will increase. You're a business and this is what businesses do. Of course you have to honor any current contracts or agreements, but once those are complete, implement your new rate. Try to do this about a month in advance so they have plenty of notice, and if you get pushback, you have time to seek out new clients. I know the thought of sending an email like this makes you want to ball up in a corner. Fun fact: None of my clients have pushed back when I used this approach. Go get your money!

Pay yourself first

Growing up, the biggest priority in my household was to pay bills. I adopted this same approach with my own finances as an adult. I never thought to set aside money for myself, even if it meant having pennies to my name after bills were taken care of. Depending on what responsibilities and family obligations you have, bill collectors are just a few of the people your hard-earned money goes to. As more Black women become the breadwinners of our families, we have to financially support everyone from parents and siblings, to children and partners.

When you're taking care of everyone else, the thought of keeping money for yourself sounds impossible. I'm here to tell you it is *very* possible. And if you're looking to progress financially, it's non-negotiable. The first step is to open a savings account separate from your regular checking account. Name the account after yourself, name it "Me, Myself, and I," or whatever reminds you this money is for you only. Then set up an automatic transfer to this account every time you get paid, even if it's $5. As it grows, use it to make a purchase just for you, like a professional development course, vacation, or spa day. Bills are a constant in life, but there's only one you. Before taking care of everyone else, take care of yourself first.

FIVE

I JUST WANT TO BE SUCCESSFUL

The road to success as a business owner is rocky, especially in the early days. And when a successful entrepreneur tells the story of how they got to where they are, it usually comes with dramatic anecdotes. Like the time they moved to a big city with $20 to their name, or worked on their business until early morning and went without sleep before clocking in at their day job.

The rags-to-riches stories are the ones we can't get enough of, but they gloss over some important details. Like the seemingly unlimited amount of free labor expected of would-be entrepreneurs to prove themselves as they build momentum. The idea is to offer your skills at a deep discount upfront, in exchange for exposure that hopefully leads to paid opportunities later. I started to question this practice in my early days of journalistic work, where it's standard to request interviews from subject matter experts for feature stories. I made it my mission to seek out Black women for interviews, many of them entrepreneurs, since I noticed the prevalence of white male opinions across all journalistic pieces.

Still, I felt guilty asking Black women to take out time in

their schedules to speak with me at no cost. They juggled duties as mothers and wives, along with businesses and sometimes day jobs. I turned down interview requests in the past because I couldn't afford time away from paid freelance work, so I knew what it was like from both sides. While talking to another journalist friend, she mentioned a similar experience when she wanted to interview a Black woman for a piece covering the Buddhist community. Because Black women Buddhist leaders rarely get to share their experience on a large platform, she hoped to include a unique perspective. When she reached out for quotes, the woman she wished to interview requested compensation. After my friend relayed the request to her colleagues, they balked at the idea of paying for an interview.

For years the journalism industry has deemed it unethical to compensate experts for interviews, due to potential conflicts of interest. What's ignored is the layer of privilege in unpaid interviews with major media outlets. When you identify as a person of color, woman, or LGBTQ+, among other underrepresented communities, you don't have the luxury to give away knowledge for free. You probably work a 9-to-5, freelance, or both to make ends meet. Prior to our culture's increasing interest in diversity, upper-class white people (think: doctors, lawyers, CEOs) were the go-to experts, who could afford to volunteer an hour of time without significant financial repercussions. While the media and other companies now seek diverse voices, those diverse voices don't have the means to give an interview several times a month with no pay.

This aspect of networking makes it difficult for Black women entrepreneurs to grow connections in the same meaningful way as our white counterparts. The unpaid internships and fellowships with a $1,000 monthly stipend in cities like New York and D.C. are laughably impractical when your basic living expenses are double that amount. If you're not white, rich, and well-connected, you'll miss out on opportunities because you don't have the privilege to drop everything for months of unpaid—or low-paying—work. In this chapter, I highlight the trial and error that comes with getting a business off the ground for Black women, and share resources for you to get the support you need.

Troubles magnified by a pandemic

I discussed the systemic barriers in mentorship and networking with Nia*, a Diversity, Equity, and Inclusion strategist and career coach.[1] As a business owner and Black woman, Nia knows firsthand the challenge to gain access to opportunities that move your business forward.

"The biggest issue I recognize is the lack of information on *how* to get resources as Black business owners," she told me. "When I say resources, I mean the monetary side, knowing where to go when you need funding. And once you find those sources, how do you position yourself to get that funding?"

The lack of funding for Black entrepreneurs is more apparent since the onset of the COVID-19 pandemic. When small businesses were forced to close physical locations due to public health concerns, they faced tough financial decisions, like how to pay building rent and whether to lay off staff until they reopened. While the United States government released more than $349 billion of funds to small business owners in March 2020, loopholes in relief initiatives like the Paycheck Protection Program (PPP) left people of color and women empty-handed. It was estimated that more than 90 percent of businesses owned by people of color were shut out of the program.[2] This was partly because the loans were approved the quickest for businesses that already had a standing relationship with major lenders. Once funds ran out, this left business owners without prior banking history, back at square one.

It also highlighted the flawed logic that banks would take

the risk of lending money to new customers at the peak of a historic economic downturn. If they required impeccable credit history during peaceful times, what incentive did they have to extend financing to small business owners struggling to stay above water? Black business owners discussed their frustrations with the confusing PPP application process, in online forums. Meanwhile, white business owners shared that their lawyers and accountants walked them through the process to eventually be approved for funding. Left without adequate assistance in a crisis, Black entrepreneurs fell another step behind in the ongoing journey to maintain a thriving business.

Taking a test without the answers

Pre-pandemic factors influence Black business owners' chances to secure investors, some we're aware of but unable to prove. Unfortunately, we've learned that Black startup founders receive less than one percent of all venture capital funding.[3] According to data gathered by ProjectDiane 2018, a biennial study on the state of Black women founders, the average amount of funding raised by Black women-owned startups is $42,000.[4] Black women-led startups raised $289 million in venture capital from 2009 to 2017. That sounds like a lot of money...until you factor in that this represents 0.06 percent of an estimated $424.7 billion (yes, with a "b") in total venture capital investments during the same time.[5] Plus, Black business owners often come from a different background than the wealthy white men who might invest in our ideas. Because of this, we can be rejected for any reason, from the way we wear our hair to the language we use.

Nia mentioned this: "I had a conversation once about names and how a name that's 'too Black' can deter a potential investor due to bias. That's one of many systemic issues Black business owners face."

This reminds me of when a colleague introduced me and my ex to her spouse. He, a white man, casually said, "Oh, your name (my ex's) is way easier to say than Quinisha." Black women deal with this shit all the time, even in business settings. We carry the extra burden to make our names, appearance, and mannerisms "presentable" in addition to putting together a flawless sales pitch. These layers of entrepreneurship make it a challenge to get established. Knowing the right people and the right strategy, feels like taking a test everyone else has the answers to. If you don't have the answers, the road to a successful business could lead to the same dead end as your last 9-to-5.

Girls just want to have fun(ds)

Some days I wonder if a mentor is *really* what I need to move my business forward. After all, I'm clear on what I want to do and how I want to do it. I want to connect with other Black women entrepreneurs and offer resources for those in the early stages. I want to offer courses, support groups, and grant funding to make their visions come to life. When I think of it this way, I might not need a mentor at all. What I need is money. And access to spaces that keep Black women out because we don't look like the type to be successful in the business world.

We don't need a one-year fellowship or mentorship program to build on our ideas, though this is the extent of what predominantly white organizations offer in place of funding. They boast about mentorship initiatives each year, but are vague about how they'll support mentees once their time in the program comes to an end. Without ongoing (financial) support, these programs only patronize us without actually helping us move ahead. Black women don't need mentors to hold our hands. We need resources, namely funding, to make meaningful progress. We have the ideas and skills but we don't have the money, which is what keeps a business afloat. Without steady cash flow, even the most brilliant idea will always be just that—an idea.

In the absence of a strong network or financial support, Black women have to get creative when looking for guidance. It's hard to know who to trust when you're learning the ropes by yourself as an entrepreneur. Building a solid support system takes time, but it can be done with intention and strategy. Here are a few ideas for how to find the best people, and the best tools, to move your business forward.

Be vigilant of scammers

The internet is ripe with business coaches and gurus happy to offer their expertise at a cost—sometimes to the tune of several hundred or thousand dollars. This poses another problem if we shell out a lump sum of money for coaches who yield lackluster results. I asked Nia how Black women can steer clear of scams.

"Doing as much research as possible is key," she told me. " I get emails saying, 'So and so is a subject matter expert' and 'Join this webinar or masterclass' and I start with the basics. What does their website or organization look like?"

She continued: "Have they proven they actually get the results they're trying to sell me on? I'd love to connect with anyone who's used their services or products and verify they're legitimate. Not just one person, but multiple people to vouch for that expert."

Without an official mentor to guide you through entrepreneurship, insight from your peers can be equally beneficial. They can offer outside perspectives on whether an opportunity seems legit. Mentorship sounds fancy, but it basically means having someone in your corner who cares about your business goals. If you have one or two fellow entrepreneurs to lean on, it could be just the support you need.

Nia shared similar advice: "It's important to have a circle of people to rely on. They may not always have the answers, but they can connect me to someone who does. That professional community helps us protect ourselves."

With any service you consider paying for, be wary of coaches or experts who promise overnight results. If it were easy to make six figures from a business in a few weeks, everyone would be doing it. That "guaranteed success" is likely a ploy for you to buy a course with information you can find on Google. Growing your business requires some investment, but you don't have to spend tons of cash to level up—especially if it puts you in worse financial shape than before.

Have a clearly defined goal

Before you fire off that email or DM to a potential mentor, write down what you hope to gain from the relationship. Be honest about why you want a mentor and whether you've taken all the necessary steps before you reach out. It won't help you or the other person if you start off with a vague statement like "I'm stuck in my career" or "I want to own a business but don't know where to start."

Remember: A mentor's job is to guide you, not do your work for you. Do your homework and make sure you've covered the basics before you ask for help. If you've tried everything you can think of to make progress in a specific area, share those details with your prospective mentor so they know you've laid the groundwork. A mentorship is most useful when you have a clear idea of what you want to accomplish and how a mentor can help you reach your goals. If you aren't clear about what you want or where you need to go, that's okay. It also means you might not be ready to solicit the assistance of a mentor yet. Instead, channel that energy into figuring out your next steps. Write out a list of your values, skills, and experience. Read books and articles that cover your topics of interest to get a better understanding of how other people in your industry address them. What do they say that you like? What's missing that you think you can help with?

Then come up with a few goals you can reach within the next couple months. If your goal is to grow your email list, consistently create content for your audience every week or two weeks. If you want to build your presence as an authority on a platform like LinkedIn, commit to posting at least one to two helpful articles in your industry regularly. Keep a journal or other documentation of what you do and what the results are. Growing in your professional life is a process and just because you don't see results right away, doesn't mean you've failed. And even if you do fail, that's more information to help you readjust and improve.

NOW THAT WE'VE covered what to look for in a mentor, what if you can't find anyone who's a good match? While it's nice to have a trusted mentor rooting for you, don't give into the hype that you can't run a successful business without one. I'll let you in on a little secret: I've never had an official mentor since I started working for myself. I filled in the gaps by following other entrepreneurs online, participating in webinars, and getting involved in different communities. If I get stuck or have a question, most people I've connected with are more than happy to help me figure out a solution.

Even if you have a great mentor, the direction and success of your business is ultimately up to you. The beauty of entrepreneurship is that it can look however you want it to. While a mentor can give you a detailed blueprint of exactly how they built their business, there's no guarantee you'll get the same results. Too much reliance on doing things the way your mentor does, will take the focus away from the unique vision you offer. Because I always advocate for having a Plan B, here are some strategies on how to be your own mentor.

Make Google (and the library) your friend

Although Google isn't always the most accurate information source, it gives you a head start on research. As you look into topics of interest, try what's known as "The CRAAP Test" to vet sources.[6] CRAAP is an acronym for Currency, Relevance, Authority, Accuracy, and Purpose. When you read a blog post or article, consider how timely the information is (currency). Does it give you the information you need (relevance)? Then take a close look at the author's credentials (authority) and whether they have the level of knowledge to give useful advice. Next, can the information be supported with evidence (accuracy)? Does the author provide statistics to back up information, or are they stating an opinion? Finally, think about the purpose of the content. Is it meant to inform, entertain, or persuade its audience? This method helps you weed out a lot of the shady takes floating around the internet.

And while blog posts are helpful, nothing beats a good book for a deep dive into business and professional development. The library is a resource we forget to use in this Google-dependent era. You can check out multiple books at once (for free!) to learn more about your area of interest. Knowledge is power, and I can't think of a better investment than to arm yourself with as much of it as possible.

Put your knowledge into practice

While knowledge is power, the information you consume from a book or online course is only useful if you apply what you learn in real time. The eagerness to always learn is sometimes a disguise for procrastination. Like signing up for five business webinars every month instead of reaching out to potential clients. That time you spend in online workshops is time away from growing other parts of your business. Being an entrepreneur is a challenge and it's scary to move into uncharted territory. However, you stifle your growth if you spend too much time listening to every business guru who pops up.

Be intentional in applying what you learn to push your business ahead. If you take a course that shares 50-plus ways to market your services, choose at least ten of those strategies to implement for a few months before you sign up for another course. If your social media profiles are good to go, skip that webinar on how to optimize your LinkedIn page and strike up a conversation with someone from your target audience. Find out their likes, dislikes, and what you can offer to make you stand out from your competition. As you exercise your entrepreneurial muscles in real life, you'll gain knowledge just as valuable as what you'd learn in a class—if not more.

Take a chance on yourself

I once posted a question online for opinions on whether investing in yourself means spending money, and I got a lot of great responses. One person pointed out that sometimes taking a leap of faith is the best way to invest in yourself. It's a simple observation, but one we don't value as much as we should. I've taken numerous leaps of faith in my life, like leaving the military, moving cross-country to California, and quitting my job, to name a few. I didn't think about it at the time, but these investments improved my wellbeing. Taking a chance on yourself is what helps you reach your best potential. It doesn't always feel that way when you're going through the motions, but if you don't take a chance on yourself, who will?

SIX
SAME SHIT, DIFFERENT (WORK) DAY

"You haven't actually told me what you do or the value you've brought to your clients, and that's typically a conversation that is had well before hiring and paying an upfront consulting fee. If you have examples of your work to send over, then I may indeed hire you. But I simply can't pay $200 when I don't even know what I'm paying for."

This response came from a content director at a lending company after I inquired where to send my invoice for a pending discovery call. She sent me a direct message via Twitter a week earlier because of a tweet I wrote about distaste for editors who whitewash my work. This was during the aftermath of George Floyd's murder and subsequent protests. Several editors commissioned me to write about race and diversity, only to make edits that neutralized the seriousness of racial disparities in the United States. I was disappointed, but not surprised, that even at the peak of racial tension across the country, editors opted to appease their white audience.

The content director's company was putting together a diversity initiative to be more inclusive in their writing, and she wanted to know if I had additional information. I told her I'd be happy to share resources, along with my consulting fees, and followed up with an email a few days later. She suggested a day and time for a chat and I asked where to send my invoice, resulting in her confusion over what she should pay for. I responded with a reminder that *she* had reached out to *me*. I added that I'm an independent contractor who charges for my time and expertise, and if she bothered to do any research prior to contacting me, she would know exactly what I do. Then I indulged my petty side and blocked her.

This wasn't the first time a potential client scoffed at the idea of paying for my time, but it never gets any less insulting. I've lost count of the brands and publications who reached out with requests to "hop on a quick call" and "pick my brain" without mention of compensation. They do so casually, with lots of exclamation marks, as if I should be excited for the opportunity to provide unpaid labor. The irony isn't lost on me that most of these companies reach out as part of their efforts to increase awareness around diversity. That they don't think twice about asking a Black woman to give her time for free, is an example of how deeply rooted white entitlement is. In these moments, I'm reminded that entrepreneurship is still subject to the same foolishness from white folks as the workplace.

I technically have the power to walk away, but the stakes are higher for me than a company with more money and resources. Once I turn them down, they can easily find another writer to work for pennies or share their ideas at no cost. I, on the other hand, have the task of seeking out better clients, which takes weeks or months in the best-case scenario. Though I'm not an employee, the mental and physical exhaustion of having to prove my value to client prospects, isn't much different from what I experienced at past jobs. While entrepreneurship comes with more freedom than a day job, it doesn't eliminate the disparities of racism and sexism in American culture. Black women have to battle the same gatekeepers from the workplace with the power to hinder our business growth. I'll share insight on what brings "same shit, different day" energy to entrepreneurship, and wrap up with strategies to help you grow your business despite the obstacles.

The push to amplify Black voices

Major corporations are eager to notice Black entrepreneurs in the aftermath of highly publicized racial violence. It mirrors behavior in the workplace, when managers delegate diversity projects to the one Black employee on the team, simply because they're Black. In the summer of 2020, I was flooded with emails from companies that wanted to amplify Black voices during the reawakening of the Black Lives Matter movement. While it was a welcome change to receive inbound requests rather than send letters of interest into a void, I couldn't shake the discomfort that these opportunities only came as a result of another Black person's murder. Although I knew *they* knew they were suddenly interested in my work because of the color of my skin, what could I say? When business opportunities for Black women are scarce under the best circumstances, a simultaneous pandemic and recession hardly felt like the time to turn away work, even if the motives were problematic.

This dilemma for Black entrepreneurs was highlighted by *The New York Times* in a piece titled "A Rush to Use Black Art Leaves the Artists Feeling Used."[1] Black creative professionals, most of them self-employed, shared stories of brands looking to collaborate in the weeks following George Floyd's murder. Shantell Martin described an invitation from an advertising company to create a Black Lives Matter mural on Microsoft's Fifth Avenue storefront in New York City. The email included a line asking if Martin could complete the project within a few days, while protests for justice were "still relevant."

Martin and a group of other Black artists wrote an open

letter to Microsoft and its advertising agency McCann, describing disappointment at the language in the email and its priority of brand messaging over the seriousness of another devastating loss in the Black community. Chief executives from Microsoft and McCann later made public apologies to Martin online. The email was just one insensitive gesture from companies in their attempts to portray solidarity with Black folks. Artists like Martin were asked to give input on diversity initiatives, without compensation for their time and expertise. Others, like queer influencer Lydia Okello, were offered free clothing from companies like Anthropologie in exchange for social media content during Pride month. When they shared their rates with the producer who reached out, their requests for payment were ignored.

"I've worked as a Black creative all my adult life, and I've noticed that there's often an assumption that you should feel flattered that this large company is reaching out to you, that it has noticed you, and that reflects a greater cultural narrative that the creative work of marginalized groups is less valuable," Okello said. Anthropologie's parent company, URBN, later said in a statement that it handled the "overture to Lydia poorly."

These incidents display the hypocrisy of companies that holler "Black Lives Matter" while using Black professionals for cool points and paying us pennies. The lip service about equity is cute, but it rings hollow when media attention fades on police brutality against the Black community, and corporate interest in Black voices fades along with it. Much like a 9-to-5, once a company takes its share of our creative and intellectual property, we're left with little more than the temporary high of their fleeting admiration. And as entrepreneurs, the same bills because collectors don't accept a big-name brand's admiration as payment.

"I'm speaking"

American culture has a long history of speaking over Black women. The world got a front-row view of this inequity during the 2020 vice presidential debate between former vice president Mike Pence and Kamala Harris, who would go on to win the vice presidency in November. While both candidates were slotted two minutes to talk about pressing political topics, Pence continued to go over his time and interrupt Harris during her responses. With no input from debate moderator, *USA Today's* Washington Bureau Chief Susan Page, Harris stated with a smile, politely but firmly, "Mr. Vice President, I'm speaking."[2]

In "The Significance of 'I'm Speaking'" published by *The Root*, Maiysha Kai dissected the racial and gendered undertones of the debate and the power dynamics at play.[3] The three individuals in the room represented what we see in everyday professional settings: "[T]he white man emboldened by his presumption of place; the woman of color dutifully if begrudgingly playing by the prescribed rules to fight the good fight against tyranny, and the 53 percent of white women too cowed by their proximity to white male power to do the right and rational thing in respect for the greater good."

Further, while women of all ethnic backgrounds related to Harris' simple but poignant statement, the moment reflected the average Black woman's life experience. Kai pointed out, "Page's passivity echoed the largest failure of white feminism, which, for all its altruism, has unfailingly centered whiteness, first and foremost. That Harris should have to reclaim her time from the person tasked with keeping it echoed the ways in which Black feminists have been forced to reimagine and reclaim a liberation movement we helped build."

The observation of white women's failure at allyship brought flashbacks of my own "I'm speaking" moments during past work conflicts. When a white woman cut me off in a meeting or neglected to give me appropriate credit for an idea, I voiced my disapproval. I made a deliberate attempt to be as non-threatening as possible, using "I feel" and "In my opinion" statements. Alas, the outcome never changed. Rather than pause and listen, each white woman offered a hasty apology and centered her own fragility. The conversation shifted from the issue at hand, to her struggle to be understood by people of color. Once this happened, I knew any chance of a productive dialogue was out the window. And while these encounters diminished once I left the workplace, I still fight to be heard as an entrepreneur.

The week after George Floyd's murder, an editor asked me to write a piece on Black women and the financial disparities we face in America. She wanted a quick turnaround—three days to be exact. I agreed to take it on and turned in a draft within the requested time frame. The editor sent feedback a few days later that didn't sit well with me. I got the sense she wanted me to overexplain the disparities Black women experience, and provide "proof" when most discrimination against us is subtle. Plus, she humblebragged about her years-long desire to explore this topic, confirming my suspicions that the Black community's plights are only deemed important when white people say so.

NORMALLY I WOULD SUCK it up and make the revisions to get it over with, but not this time. I pushed back on the edits and shared concerns about her attempt to tone down the subject matter. She asked me to call her so we could work through my concerns. I made a list of points to help me stay on topic during our chat. Within minutes of getting on the call, I was barely halfway through the list before she interjected, apologizing profusely and promising to do whatever it took to make it right. I sighed quietly as I realized this would be a repeat of conversations with white women at past jobs. Instead of trying to reach common ground on the complexities of race, I asked for clarity on editorial details and ended the conversation as quickly as I could. After the call, I submitted revisions and waited to hear back. The piece was never published.

I gave myself credit for speaking up, but was frustrated by the editor's lack of awareness, followed by ghosting on an "important" piece. Similar to my experience as an employee, her carelessness silenced my voice. Seeking to explain this to businesses desperate to prove their interest in racial justice, is usually a futile cause. And unlike a 9-to-5 with an HR department that at least *pretends* to be neutral, entrepreneurs don't have a third party to back us up. We can pursue legal action if we suspect foul play, but that takes time and resources we don't have. And most companies know that. This puts us in the same position of dispirited silence we endured as employees.

I'd love to have a perfectly packaged solution for how to navigate the sexism and racism that comes with entrepreneurship as a Black woman, but I still haven't figured it out. I've had times when I took on a project I felt uneasy about, simply because rent was due and I needed the check. The best I can offer is to let other Black women know you're not alone. When you negotiate with a company to get a higher rate and they say there's no room in the budget, it's not because you weren't confident enough. When you push back on a brand that wants to pick your brain and shudders at the audacity of your request for compensation, you're not doing the most. You're operating business the way you should, and systemic racism, capitalism, and patriarchy will never fail to hit you with the fuckery.

You have to pick your battles. If you're unapologetically Black and proud, of course you should turn down a brand that subscribes to an "All Lives Matter" rhetoric. On the other hand, you might have to swallow your pride and deal with the client who thinks they're woke but says awkward shit on a Zoom call. It doesn't make you a sellout. These are the cards we've been dealt and we have to play our hands accordingly. As you grow your business and visibility, you'll have more power over the clients you can afford to turn down. You're doing the best you can under the circumstances—while building your own empire. In the meantime, here are tips to help you navigate situations that bring back memories from the 9-to-5 life.

Always have receipts

You're probably familiar with the term "C.Y.A." (Cover Your Ass) in the workplace to always keep documentation in the event of drama. The same rules apply when you work with clients independently. I prefer to communicate with most of my clients via email, but if they request a Zoom or phone call, I send a follow-up email to what we discussed on the call.

Here's a follow-up email I sent to another client after a call to address my concerns about the direction of a project:

Hi [name],

It was a pleasure to finally "meet" you over Zoom this week. I wanted to send a quick follow-up to our conversation for reference when we reconnect after my time off during the first week of August.

Since working on our first piece together, I shared that it would be helpful for me if you leave comments on drafts so I have a better understanding on the direction of the piece. You mentioned that you value open dialogue throughout the editing process, which I will be sure to keep in mind.

You shared that [company] is looking for "ideas-based" stories that are universal and not overly niche. I will send over ideas that best align with this type of content moving forward. We also touched base on the payment terms for my last piece which is Net-30 from the date of publishing, usually paid at the end of the month. If you can confirm

this, that would be great. Thanks again for reaching out and I look forward to working together again in the near future. Talk soon!

Keeping receipts helps when and if miscommunications arise. It also saves you time for similar conversations with future clients. Rather than try to figure out the right wording all over again, you can use prior emails as a template and plug in new details as needed.

Take your time

After the client who asked me to turn in a piece within three days, I decided to be more cautious of people who want quick turnarounds on deliverables. Quick money sounds good in the beginning, but there are usually underlying factors that make it less than ideal. As business owners, sometimes we think we have to act fast so we don't miss out on opportunities. What's meant for you is for you and there's no need to rush anything.

If a brand or company puts pressure on you to make a quick decision, that's a red flag. Folks who have their shit together and care about quality work, will take as much time as they need to get things right. Ask them what they're looking to accomplish from the work they want you to do. Why are they interested in working with you? Is this a one-off project or do they want to form a long-term partnership? Get clear details about the scope of the work, rates, and the accounting process. You don't want to spend more time chasing down payment than it takes to complete the project. Taking your time requires a little more work upfront, but it beats the alternative of rushing into a decision you regret in the end.

Save the free game for yourself

Maybe due to the informal real-time interaction normalized by social media, brands now reframe business transactions into "getting to know you" calls. Instead of using the words "consultation" or "meeting," it's common to hear terms like "quick call" or "chat over coffee." My spidey senses tell me these informal phrases are a sneaky strategy to skate around the discussion of payment. These brands present themselves as fans of your work or friends. And friends don't charge friends for a quick call, right?

Wrong. Any business that reaches out to you for help, whether it's for their social media marketing, content strategy, or hiring practices, is requesting a service. Regardless of how friendly or informal it sounds, they're asking you to perform labor you don't owe if they don't pay you. Your next question might be, "How do you network/bring in clients/expand your reach if you don't hop on a quick call?" Easy. Reserve your time and resources for the people who are serious about paying for what you offer. That 30-minute call you spend with a company you'll never hear from again? Could be an e-book you sell to customers at $20 a pop. Those sample slides you put together so a client lead can see if your work fits the tone of their brand? Could be part of a presentation you pitch to a conference for a paid speaking gig.

The magic of being an entrepreneur is that you can get as creative as you want to grow your business. Marketing isn't about spending hours on calls with folks who want to test the waters for their half-assed idea. If they're not sure what they're looking for, chances are they won't be a good client to work with anyway. Your job as a business owner is not to do your client's research for them at no cost. Your expertise is valuable, otherwise they wouldn't have approached you in the first place. Keep that in mind, and carry yourself like the boss you are.

Cue Kelis' "Bossy" intro

SEVEN

PUTTING ON A BRAVE FACE

"How are you doing with the coronavirus hysteria going on?"

The text came from my dad just as self-quarantine advisories were ramping up, and a couple days prior to COVID-19 officially being declared a national emergency.

"I'm doing well," I wrote back. I shared that I was trying not to give in to the panic and told him to be safe. Actually, I was already panicked. My bank account was depleted after paying bills for the month, and I had more than $2,000 of outstanding invoices from freelance work. I was low on toiletries and debated using my credit card to stock up. Two days later, another text came from my dad, asking again if I needed anything. I finally admitted I could use help with buying supplies. The world was literally in a state of emergency, yet I felt obligated to handle things on my own. In the face of extreme adversity, I've suffered silently rather than accept help from others. I've noticed similar behavior in my friends and family, all Black women who refrain from getting support when they need it the most.

While being strong and resilient is worn as a badge of honor, it compounds the physical and mental stress of taking on too much. In *The New York Times* Op-ed "The Strong and Stressed Black Woman," clinical psychologist Dr. Inger Burnett-Zeigler explores the inner turmoil Black women go through to put on a brave face.[1] Dr. Burnett-Zeigler describes the strong Black woman as a "cultural icon, born of [B]lack women's resilience in the face of systemic oppression that has dismantled families and made economic stability a formidable challenge. She is self-sufficient and self-sacrificing. She is a provider, caretaker and homemaker. And often, she is suffering."

She goes on to share her experience providing therapy to other Black women, who are embarrassed to solicit her services, and only do so when they're overwhelmed with life and "can't take it anymore." While the world applauds strong Black women, the mental and physical toll of being strong is significant. Compared to white women, Black women experience higher levels of stress as a result of family obligations, finances, discrimination, and safety concerns related to living in neighborhoods with high crime rates. Black women are more likely to suffer from depression, with severe and long-lasting symptoms that interfere with our daily lives. Despite this, more than 16 percent of Black women are uninsured and can't afford necessary mental health treatment. This leads to other coping mechanisms like overeating and drug and alcohol abuse. The stress and depression can also bring long-term physical health issues, such as diabetes, obesity, and high blood pressure.

These are just a few of the problems stacked against Black women *before* the onset of a pandemic. Once COVID-19 swept the country, it came with a slew of devastating effects that hit everyone hard, especially Black women. Most restaurants and retail stores shut down for months at a time, which directly impacted Black women, who are more likely to work in these industries. After several weeks of tracking the spread of the virus, the Centers for Disease Control (CDC) reported a disproportionately higher number of deaths in Black and Latinx communities than white counterparts.[2] Schools and daycares abruptly closed, leaving single parents alone with the burden of finding alternative childcare options, predominantly people of color. With so many emotional and financial hardships taking place at once, this was another striking reminder of why we should reframe the idea that Black women must carry our burdens alone.

Social media struggles

As if being a strong Black woman isn't hard enough, now that we live in a fast-paced digital world, there's more pressure to be on top of your game—or at least make it look that way. When your peers constantly share their wins online, it sends an unspoken message that there is no room for failure, even as a new entrepreneur. Before our unlimited access to the internet, you could be blissfully unaware of your rivals' accomplishments. These days you can immediately log onto any social media platform and watch as they share "personal news" about five-figure contracts, book deals, and major brand partnerships. Even if you're fairly confident, it's damn near impossible to suppress the wave of envy. You'll always find someone in your industry who appears to be doing better than you.

But as a strong Black woman, you'd rather chew on a handful of chocolate-covered crickets than admit your business is struggling when Instagram tells you everyone else is killing it. So you keep quiet as you face challenges in your personal and professional life. You post selfies of your fiercest makeup beat with the caption #blessed, even if you spent the last night in tears because your client hasn't paid your invoice and you don't know how you're going to pay rent. You share lengthy Twitter threads with some of your best tips for success as an entrepreneur, when most of the time you don't know what the fuck you're doing.

It's nothing to be embarrassed of. I've done it all the time, and still do. I was going through a whole divorce and shared articles with my audience about how to manage money and careers. I believe this is how social media was designed, to keep us tied to the obligation of being "on" at all times. When you're building a brand, you have to present your best self to the world. And it's hard to present your best self when you're worried about how to afford household supplies this week or trying to process a divorce all on your own. The perfectionist culture of social media only reinforces the other cultural expectation for Black women to be strong and independent.

I follow and interact with other amazing Black women online who launched startups, freelanced for several years, and carved out their own lane after they reached a dead end in the workplace. All while juggling family responsibilities, friendships, and speaking about flaws in the entrepreneurial space. Their dopeness is inspiring, but it triggers my insecurities.

Business is slowly picking up, while bills roll in like clockwork. The hustle of entrepreneurship is exciting yet time consuming. *Should I launch a product to bring in passive income, like a course or e-book?* I wonder. *Maybe...but will people like it? Do people really care what I have to say? It would suck to take the time and energy to put behind a physical product, only for it to flop. Should I do a survey or poll to gauge interest? Do I need a business coach?*

I have this never-ending inner monologue with myself on a daily basis, despite how many milestones I've reached in my life. Serving in the military is something only about one percent of this country will ever do.[3] Even though I hated it most of the time, it allowed me the opportunity to travel to other countries, including Croatia, Bahrain, and Dubai. Military service helped me reach yet another goal: To obtain my bachelor's degree without taking on more student loan debt. I landed my job in California two months after I graduated, and when I told people I applied without any personal connections to the company and received an offer after virtual interviews only, they jokingly said I was a unicorn. While the job didn't work out, it moved me into the next stage of my career as a freelancer, and a few months into full-time self-employment, I wrote my first article for *The New York Times*. Despite all of this, I still tell myself it's nothing compared to what I see on my Twitter newsfeed. I don't think that's an accident. The human brain is no match for technology that offers an endless reel of everyone else's carefully curated lives.

As stressful as social media is, it's the foundation of my freelance writing career. If I hadn't joined the personal finance community on Twitter, I never would have met my freelance writing coach, who invited me to events where I connected with other freelancers. I wouldn't have come across pitch calls for major media outlets like *USA Today* and *Medium*, and I wouldn't have the platform to share content from my blog. Like most Black women I know, the traditional path to building a meaningful career hasn't worked out for me. I never had the privilege of going to a fancy journalism school or knowing someone who knows someone who could get me a sweet writing gig with a prestige publication. I cold pitched ideas to get my writing on blogs with a bigger audience, and when all I got was radio silence, I turned those pitches into my own blog posts. Being active online helped me share my voice with a larger audience and I've met amazing people because of it. Sometimes I wonder what it would be like if social media wasn't such a big factor in my work as a writer—especially when this space glorifies the Strong Black Woman rhetoric.

Black women will save us

Public racial tension puts pressure on Black women to speak up even as we're processing traumatic events, like the murder of Breonna Taylor and subsequent verdict that failed to hold the offending police offers accountable. As "influencers," we need to have a hot take on every topic surrounding race and diversity, in addition to running our businesses. It's a heavy burden, especially when non-Black counterparts are free to opt out of these uncomfortable discussions and share their regularly scheduled posts with marketing strategies and best social media practices.

When we do speak out, there's an insatiable demand from—usually white—followers to give them more. White allies pressure you to tell them how to support the Black community. If you're excited about books coming out in the next year by Black women authors, they ask you to share a list so they can read those books, too. These are some examples from seemingly well-intentioned white folks who see themselves as different from "other" people. In actuality, their sense of entitlement to emotional labor from Black women is the same racism cloaked in the guise of someone who wants to learn more and show solidarity. Social media is good for connecting, but the downside for Black women is the expectation to be anti-racism consultants for strangers.

Black women are upheld as pillars of strength and the go-to players whenever shit hits the fan. When a company faces criticism for its lack of diversity, it's not long before there's a public announcement that a Black woman is now their Chief Diversity Something or Other. After United States Senator Kamala Harris was named as Joe Biden's running mate in the 2020 presidential election, Mexican politician Jorge Guajardo posted on Twitter, "Black women will save the United States."[4]

Immediately, the tweet received a flood of responses from Black women with rebuttals on how demoralizing and misguided this statement actually is. A user with the handle @FreshWithDepth responded, "Yall [sic] don't pay us equally. Don't promote us within your organizations. Don't credit us for our ideas or style or impact. Don't allow us the space or outlets to celebrate or uplift ourselves. WHY should we save anyone?"[5] Good question. After all, why are Black women only called on when the world is on fire? We share our opinions and expertise, and get constant pushback. Once white institutions go through with poorly planned strategies and encounter inevitable backlash, they turn to Black women to swoop in and save the day. It's a modern version of the "mammy" role Black women are compelled to take on. We're held to the expectation that we should immediately and selflessly sacrifice ourselves for the greater good.

Malcolm X said it best: "The most disrespected person in America is the Black woman. The most unprotected person in America is the Black woman. The most neglected person in America is the Black woman." Black women take on the burdens of partners, family members, friends, employers, and entire governments. Yet when we need protection, the rest of the world turns its back on us. We bear criticism for our hair, skin color, sexuality, religious beliefs (or lack thereof), and everything in between. We're told we're too bossy, too loud, too quiet, too sexy, not sexy enough, too sensitive, too opinionated. Everyone loves to snap and say "yasss queen" when we entertain them or come up with a cool new dance or catchphrase, but no one sees us as actual human beings. They love us as long as we're fun and sassy in a non-threatening manner. That changes once we speak out about racism and sexism, and demand to be treated as equal for the blood, sweat, and tears we've put into everything we do.

TRAGEDIES, like the deaths of Sandra Bland and Breonna Taylor, reinforce that reality in a vivid and painful way. I get chills when I see their photos because they remind me of myself. They had hopes, dreams, flaws, opinions, and hobbies. That they've been reduced to hashtags and memes, fills me with an indescribable rage. These tragedies could happen to me. I served five years in the military for a country that wouldn't blink an eye if I turned up dead or missing. The fact that the same country wants me to save it, but refuses to acknowledge me until a crisis is an insult. During times like this, I don't want to be strong. I don't want to be the superhero who saves the day. I want to lay in bed and cry for all the Black women who deserve so much more. I want someone to protect me from the evil that lurks around every corner. Being strong and resilient has never been a problem for me. I have another dilemma, which is that I don't know how *not* to be strong. I don't know how *not* to be independent. I don't know how to ask for help. And that's a hard pill to swallow.

When someone asks how I'm doing, my default response is, "I'm fine." I've mastered the art of putting on a brave face, even when I'm going through a deep episode of depression. Any time I'm faced with a tough decision, my instinct is to figure it out, rather than seek support. By the time I share my true feelings with anyone, I've endured the loneliness and turmoil of working through it on my own. It's an unhealthy coping mechanism and one I still don't know how to unlearn.

I spoke with a friend years ago about songs like Beyoncé's "Run the World (Girls)" and the irony that Black girls and women really *don't* run the world. In a way we do, but we don't get nearly the amount of recognition we deserve for it. Like when we lend marketing ideas to companies that want to tap into our demographic's buying power, or take the lead in voter registration efforts during a crucial election season. We're constantly hit with #blackgirlmagic hashtags that imply we're unfazed by inequities due to race and gender.

The idea of #blackgirlmagic perpetuates that it's okay to abuse and mistreat Black women because we're strong enough to handle it. We don't get the same grace as white women and other women of color because the assumption is we can handle all the nastiness the world throws at us. We're independent not because we want to be, but because we don't have a choice. When I think of it this way, it doesn't feel magical. It feels toxic, depressing, and draining. It feels like the world has failed us. I'd like to see Black women try a different approach. Rather than jump into action in the instance of racial injustice or a company's diversity snafu, let's sit some discussions out.

We've been calling out racism, microaggressions, and inhumane treatment for centuries. If we never shared our experiences with discrimination again, there would still be a million resources available for the white folks desperate to be educated whenever anti-racism is trending. Most Black women I know are strong, resilient, and self-sufficient. While I love this about us, I want us to embrace the moments when we're not strong. I want us to be okay with not having all the answers. And look out for ourselves before we look out for everyone else. The fight for equality is far from over. We won't have the strength to fight if we burn out because of the outdated trope to carry the weight of the world on our shoulders. It won't be easy, so here are a few practical ways to resist the urge to be strong on and offline.

Celebrate your wins *and* losses—privately

It's hard to grow a business in a culture that focuses on constant wins. We're all at different points in our entrepreneurship journey, and you might feel pressured to be at the level of someone with 10 more years in the game. Regardless of what everyone else is doing, the only person you need to compete with is yourself. It's easier said than done, but it's the best way to focus on where you want to be instead of where you *think* you should be. If you used to get a few hundred monthly views on your blog and now you're up to a few thousand, celebrate that shit. If you started out with five Youtube subscribers and now you have 50, toot your own horn.

Likewise, if your blog, podcast, or Youtube channel hasn't grown the way you hoped by now, celebrate anyway. In a world of instant gratification, sometimes we think our business growth will go from 0 to 100 within weeks or months. Your effort to learn what does or doesn't work for your business is a reason for celebration on its own. There are so many folks who talk about an idea for years and never act on it. You had an idea and took the steps to make it a reality. Don't let the illusion of social media minimize how big of a deal that is. I also recommend celebrating some of your wins and losses offline more than you do online. If something big happens in your business, whether good or bad, take a day to reflect on your feelings about it on your own. External validation is great but as an entrepreneur, it helps to process your thoughts first.

Honor the moments when you don't feel strong

Even the strongest, most resilient Black woman has days when she's tired, disappointed, and has nothing left to give. Sometimes our natural response is to immediately push past the emotions that make us feel weak because it's expected. Problem is, those feelings only resurface the next time we're hurt or disappointed. I once got an unexpected email from a well-known company about a writing project. They were looking for UX writers, a niche I didn't have experience in. The editor reached out anyway because he liked my portfolio and asked to schedule a video call for the following week. In the meantime, I researched UX writing, including the average salary for writers. To my surprise, it was a lucrative area of expertise. I hoped this might be a game-changer for my freelance income.

The day of the call, I showered, put on makeup and my favorite outfit, and turned on my charm while speaking with the editor. I told him about my background and he shared more about what they were looking for. At the end of the call, I offered to follow up with a rate quote. Before I sent the quote, I messaged a UX writer on LinkedIn for insight on the best way to propose my rates for the project. I didn't want to quote a ridiculous number and scare them off, or do the opposite and lowball myself. She offered several helpful tips, which I used to create a thorough proposal for the client. After a week of nervous anticipation, I hadn't received a response. I sent a follow-up email, and the editor broke the news that they decided to work with other writers. It wasn't my first rejection and it wouldn't be the last, but this one hit differently. I was excited to take on a new challenge since I had no prior experience in UX writing. That and the potential to move into a lucrative writing space, made me want the opportunity badly.

This was another moment when my venture to go above and beyond ended in disappointment. Normally, I would use the rejection as motivation to reach out to more UX editors in hopes to find another opportunity. This time I didn't. I closed my laptop, sat in my living room, and cried. Then I took the rest of the day off and ordered Thai food.

Black women are expected to bounce back from adversity and keep pushing. It's how we're able to leave a toxic job and start a new business a few weeks later. Even though that's the way it's always been, it doesn't have to stay that way. Allowing yourself to feel hurt and disappointment doesn't mean you've given up. Ignore the voice that says you're not cut out for entrepreneurship if you step back to process your feelings. Order your favorite takeout or binge watch a Netflix series. Call your friend for a 30-minute venting session. Before being a boss, and even before being a Black woman, you're a human being. And you deserve time and space to be human just like everyone else.

Set social media boundaries

I've met a lot of my real-life friends through social media. Still, there's another side of coin where we think of our followers as friends and lose sight of why we're on a platform in the first place. Our culture is in love with the idea of transparency and baring your soul to the internet world. The truth is that everyone who follows you is not looking out for your best interest. Just because you have thousands of followers doesn't mean you owe them a sneak peek at every detail of your life. If someone hops into your DMs and wants access to your contacts, you can say no. If followers accuse you of lying or making an exaggeration about your accomplishments, let them talk. Note: This only applies if you're being honest about what you've accomplished.

Sometimes I wonder if not sharing everything about myself online makes me a fraud. Then I think about what this would look like in a real-life situation. If I were having a private chat with a friend and a stranger walked up to put in their two cents, would I feel bad for telling them to kick rocks? Absolutely not. If they walked into my house and told me racism isn't real and I'm just playing the victim when I talk about it, would I calmly and politely share statistics to explain why they're wrong? Hell no. It's no different in an online setting. The reality is, your work won't resonate with everyone and some people are bold enough to reach out and let you know. Block, mute, or ignore anyone who oversteps your boundaries. Social media is public, but you deserve respect and safety the same as you do offline.

Disengage when you need to

In our fast-paced culture, it seems impossible to pause for self-care. I often find myself back online even after I say I need a break, for fear that too much time away will mess up my online engagement rates. Life happens though. You might be going through a breakup, loss of a loved one, or just don't feel like being around people for a while. Give a quick heads up to your social media followers, relatives, and friends that you're taking time to get some rest. You can also set up an email auto reply to let potential clients know you'll be away from your inbox and when they can expect to hear back from you. Pro tip: Add a 24-hour buffer to whatever timeline you share. For example, if you think you can respond to most emails within 48 hours, set the expectation for 72 hours to allow yourself some breathing room.

Whenever I feel guilty about stepping back for a bit, I remind myself of the saying: "You can't pour into others from an empty cup." Being an entrepreneur has always been hard, and it's even harder in the age of 24/7 communication. It seems like a symbol of success to be swamped with emails and calls, or booked for months in advance. There's nothing wrong with being booked and busy, but is it worth the damage to your own wellbeing? Give yourself grace and enjoy some quiet time every now and again. I'll end with Dr. Burnett-Zeigler's final words in her opinion piece: "Black women have harnessed their strength out of the necessity to support themselves and their families when no one else would—and that should be applauded. But there is also strength in vulnerability, comfort in seeing that you are not alone and power in knowing when to ask for help."

EIGHT

BACK IN BED WITH THE ENEMY

In a perfect world, every business would be an immediate success and make millions of dollars in revenue. However, data from the Bureau of Labor Statistics shows that nearly half (45 percent) of new businesses fail within the first five years.[1] For Black women entrepreneurs, this can be due to family issues, lack of financial resources, or changes in personal and professional goals. Some may ultimately choose to return to a 9-to-5. When this happens, mixed emotions are sure to be involved. Is a traditional job worth the trade-off of freedom? Does it make you a quitter?

These are questions I ask myself every day, especially when I complete a freelance project and have to wait 30 days to get paid. I browse through available jobs on LinkedIn and fantasize about what it would be like to show up for work and…that's it. No more hustling to find assignments. Or chasing clients for payment. Or the responsibility of making executive decisions. About 90 percent of the time, working for yourself is less about the actual work you do and more about navigating logistics of the work. These realities are rarely addressed in mainstream discussions of entrepreneurship.

I daydreamed about the perks of self-employment at previous jobs. I was tired of sitting at a desk for hours and doing repetitive work day in and day out. When I spoke to self-employed friends, they shared how liberating it was to have control over the projects they took on. That, plus the flexible schedule and freedom to work anywhere, quickly drew me into the self-employed lifestyle. Still, this is a limited view of what self-employment really looks like. Before I made a full commitment to work for myself, I tried freelancing while job hunting after graduation. Yes, I woke up when I wanted to and worked from the comfort of my living room. But aside from one client I started working with a few months before I graduated, guess how much I made after hours of researching, sending pitches, and drafting blog posts?

$0

A FEW MAGAZINES offered to pay me between $10 to $30 for 700-word articles. That meant cranking out a minimum of 10 articles a week to make $100. I couldn't justify putting in the time and effort for such a small amount of money. In spite of making no income from my first go at freelancing, bills were still due. If it weren't for savings, my last couple GI Bill payments, and my then-husband's income, life could have quickly gone bad. Self-employment sounds like sweet freedom, but with that freedom comes unpredictability. Even if you land a big contract with a client, they can back out or drag their feet in paying you. In theory, you're not "working for yourself," because your money is still in someone else's hands. You're just not going into an office Monday through Friday to get it.

Further, some companies don't realize freelancers need the same amount of money as employees—if not more. For example, I made a $60,000 annual salary at my nonprofit job, and most of my work consisted of research, writing press releases, newsletters, articles, and social media management. I use those exact skills as a freelancer, but it's common for client prospects to offer me a few hundred dollars per project and balk if I propose a higher rate. Maybe they think freelancing is something I do on the side or in between jobs, and therefore don't command the same income. Nonetheless, my bills haven't changed since I left my job, and I need enough money to live off of. The ongoing challenge to secure reliable and well-paying clients, now makes me daydream about the simplicity of a job rather than the freedom of entrepreneurship. In this chapter, I'll explore the pros and cons of going back to a 9-to-5 after self-employment, and provide tips for choosing the right company.

Crossing enemy lines?

I had a chat with Tomi, who's contemplated moving into a traditional job after freelancing for several years.[2] Tomi is the founder of mater mea, a website and community for Black women that explores the intersection of motherhood and careers. Prior to launching mater mea in 2012, Tomi worked in journalism and media, but chose to pursue freelancing after multiple experiences with discrimination and racism in traditional roles. Over the next few years, she alternated between freelance work and full-time jobs, including a position with Federated Media. She left Federated in 2015 to work on mater mea full-time. Since leaving the workplace, Tomi says her awareness around racial inequity now makes it a challenge to stay at a 9-to-5 for good.

"I've been out of an office since 2015 and since then, my racial consciousness has been raised to a point where I can't go back. Before, being around white people would be uncomfortable. There's always going to be a microaggression, or you wonder why certain things happen. The idea of having to go back to that and play office politics, and do anything other than what I want to do, is really hard for me."

Still, she admits her fear of financial insecurity plays a part in her hesitation to work on her business without the cushion of freelance income or a day job.

"Through therapy, I realized I had a limiting mindset," she shared. "I had it in my mind that I couldn't do my business full-time. If I were a different person with less fear about security, maybe I wouldn't be so quick to jump back into doing some kind of freelance work. But I'm the child of immigrants and you always have fifty-eleven jobs or one really, really good job."

I can relate, as I think a lot about money and financial stability. I love working on my own and being independent. Yet, when I'm waiting on money two months after a project wraps up, a biweekly paycheck doesn't sound so bad after all. Admitting this though, hardly fits the image of an entrepreneur who is tough, resilient, and pushes through all struggles. If you go back to a job, it feels like you're crossing enemy lines.

And in our very online world, it can be embarrassing to tell friends and family you're stepping away from self-employment. If you've been promoting your business on social media, the thought of announcing you're back at a 9-to-5 will probably be a big hit to your ego.

"Quitting entrepreneurship can make you feel like a failure, depending on how public you were about your business," Tomi said. "You feel like you have to tell people you're back at an office and that's demoralizing."

She added though, "But the people who like your posts aren't paying your bills. So there's no shame in it unless you make it shameful."

She makes a good point. Social reputation aside, I wonder whether full-time employment will be possible for myself and other Black women in the next five or ten years. One reason I started working for myself is because a stable job never felt stable. In some ways, entrepreneurship feels safer than a 9-to-5. At a full-time gig, as soon as shit goes down, you can easily get the boot and have to start job hunting all over again. Looking forward at workplace culture in its entirety, what is the ideal option for Black women to shape their careers? I posed this question to Tomi.

"It's hard to answer because not everyone wants to be an entrepreneur," she said. "I just want to do my work but I'm not interested in the business operations side, or investing the time to get good at it."

She echoes my own thoughts about the need to change our current work culture. "The virtual world shows how awful work culture is for mothers and primary caregivers. We need a complete overhaul of what we thought was propping up the world we live in."

Her words resonate strongly. The balancing act women do to maintain families and careers is unsustainable. We shouldn't *have* to pick entrepreneurship because the workplace offers no flexibility or support. Rather than put the onus on employees to choose between livelihood or sanity, employers should be held accountable for providing a healthy environment.

For example, companies should implement resources for women whose work-life balance has drastically changed due to the COVID-19 pandemic and provide childcare assistance so they remain employed. And offer programs to help employees build skills in sectors that offer more stability, like tech, health-care, and finance. Black women in particular need to be compensated fairly for our work. We also need consistent, transparent information from current and potential employers regarding salary, raises, and promotions. Only then will we start to make progress toward real equity at work. I don't know what the future holds for working Black women. I do know life happens, and there might come a day when you decide a 9-to-5 is the best fit. With that in mind, here are a few tips to help if you make the move back into corporate life.

Be vigilant of red flags

Employers often use weird euphemisms that go unnoticed when you're in desperate need of a job. A few that might sound familiar are phrases like "team player," "able to multitask," or "must be obsessed with [insert industry]."

They seem harmless enough, but what a certain type of buzzword says without actually saying, is that you'll be over-worked, underpaid, forced to deal with constant chaos, and expected to say nothing about it. If you've been self-employed for any amount of time, you're probably not about that life.

What other buzzwords should you look out for? I asked Sarah, an HR expert with 20 years of experience and creator of *The Buzz on HR* blog. She told me, "Anything in the job posting indicating a need for high tolerance for conflict, ability to work long hours, and rapid change is typically a sign the environment is problematic. Healthy work environments focus their descriptions on what the role does for the organization's overall success and what the organization's culture does for the people who work there and its community."[3]

Beyond the job description, she says to look out for red flags during the interview process, like gaslighting ("You seem too junior/senior for this role"), lack of follow-up, and obscure questions like, "If you were a bird, what kind would you be?" These are all warning signs of a disorganized and toxic culture, and you should withdraw yourself from consideration as quickly as possible.

Should you go through the entire interview process, get an offer, and you're still not feeling it, it's okay to turn the job down. I can tell you from experience, you'll never regret declining an opportunity that sets off your BS detector.

Seek out a company that aligns with your values

During the interview process, you're probably used to feeling pressure to dazzle a potential employer. You do your best to be as easygoing and accommodating as possible. If they need to change your interview time or day, you oblige without question. If you ask about company culture and they give a vague answer, you convince yourself it's not a big deal.

Remember: You should be interviewing them as much as they're interviewing you. You've juggled marketing, HR, legal, operations, and accounting all by your damn self, in addition to whatever service or product you offer. Most people won't have that kind of experience in their career. You're a valuable asset, so carry yourself accordingly.

There's no perfect job, but the job you take should be as close to perfect as you can get. Otherwise, you'll be ready to call it quits just a few months later. Ask the hard questions. Sarah said, "Ask about the company's response to the Black Lives Matter protests following the murders of George Floyd and Breonna Taylor. This will give you insight on how the company walks the talk on Diversity, Equity, and Inclusion."

She also encourages job candidates to ask questions about the company's response to the pandemic and how it supports employees with children, high health risks, or limited access to technology. Their desire—or lack thereof—to help employees succeed will let you know what the culture is like.

Companies are never shy about making sure they get what they want. You shouldn't be either. Be vocal about your needs, and if those needs can't be met, don't be afraid to turn down an offer. Even if you've decided to take a break from being your own boss, you deserve to do fulfilling work with an employer that's invested in your wellness.

Continue to hone your entrepreneurial skills

You don't have to spend all your time after work on your business, but still nurture the relationships and clientele you've developed. You worked hard to establish yourself as an entrepreneur and you should keep growing your network, even when you work for someone else.

Continue to build a rapport with other business owners and stay tuned in to industry trends. Keep at least one or two clients on the side and let them know you're still open to referrals. Stay active in online communities and share resources.

Building a business is hard and lonely, and even harder when you need it to maintain your livelihood. If you believe everything you see on social media, you might think you can only work a 9-to-5 *or* be your own boss, with no gray area. On the contrary, having a steady paycheck from a day job while you grow your own business is the best of both worlds. Don't fall for the idea that you're not a "real" entrepreneur if you have a job. Entrepreneurship looks however you want it to, so ignore the naysayers and get your money.

Whatever you decide, you can change your mind

Let's say you land a new job and decide after a few months or a year it's not for you. Or maybe you love it so much you do away with your business for good. There's no right or wrong answer for what you choose to do with your career.

Sometimes we tell ourselves if we make a decision, we have to stick it out no matter what. This is what leads to us staying in unfulfilling relationships, friendships, and career choices to avoid judgment from the world. I say it's time to normalize the real and human act of changing our minds.

What you want for your career today, probably looks much different than what you wanted 10 years ago. That's what life experience is all about. You learn new information, meet new people, and go in a new direction as a result. Don't be ashamed if you try something you thought you would like and actually hate it. Also don't be ashamed if you try something you thought you'd hate and actually love it.

It's great to crush goals as an entrepreneur or at a day job, but don't let that stop you from embracing the unknown. The unexpected twists and turns of your professional pursuits give you a unique story to share. No one pays attention to the person who stayed on a linear career path for 30-plus years. It's the folks who took risks and tried something out of the box we want to know more about.

Our brains can trick us into limiting ourselves even when we choose a different path. You'll face challenges whether you work for yourself or someone else. Don't add to that stress by sticking to a plan that no longer serves you. Whether you report to a boss or yourself, remember *you* have the final say on what your ideal career looks like.

NINE

DOES A GOLDEN TICKET EXIST?

I struggle to balance pursuing my dreams with the reality of living in a capitalist society. I want to opt out of everything and say fuck the system, but I'm not sure how to make that happen and still pay rent. In some ways, I want to be accepted by the capitalist system. Most of my life, I've worked to achieve the goal of obtaining a steady job and a nice home with the white picket fence. I can't put into words how disappointed I am to realize things will never be that easy for someone like me. It sucks to feel like I'll always have to make a trade-off between financial security and personal freedom. I've been freelance writing for two years and have yet to secure consistent income. I network, create unique content, share resources on social media, and the response feels lukewarm at best. It's exhausting to put so much consideration into my blog and online presence, to get a few "likes" here and there. I try to remind myself I'm doing the best I can, but it doesn't feel that way when my savings have dwindled and I sometimes use my credit card to cover basic expenses.

Chaotic and frustrated thoughts race through my mind

whenever another client hits me with the "We don't have the budget" line. *I want to do work I enjoy, make enough money to live comfortably, and work with clients who respect and value what I have to offer. I don't think that's asking for much, but it's so damn hard to make it a reality. I've struggled for so long and I'm tired of the struggle. I want recognition for my hard work. I deserve it. I. Fucking. Deserve. It.*

This is what entrepreneurship feels like when you don't get the world handed to you on a silver platter. You see the same advice about knowing your worth from self-employment gurus and feel sick to your stomach because you've tried those tricks and then some. Meanwhile, the world blissfully ignores the systemic issues at play and frames the lack of entrepreneurial success as a personal failure. A popular freelance writer recently claimed the easiest way to become a go-to freelancer for editors, is to turn in clean copy, meet deadlines, and do whatever you can to make the editor's job easier.

I laughed because I never miss a deadline, always turn in good copy, and have yet to land the coveted "go-to freelancer" role my white and non-Black peers boast about. So many tips around entrepreneurship are generalized and self-righteous. It's easy to tell people to charge what they're worth when you have a year of savings to keep you afloat. What about those who don't? Do they have low self-worth because they take whatever they can to pay the bills? Why do we put the burden on the most oppressed individuals of a flawed system, rather than the system itself? I'm single with no kids and live on my own so I have more room to turn down low-paying work. If my life were different, who knows how many shitty opportunities I'd have to take to provide for a family. If it's this hard to reach my goals, I wonder how hard it is for people with additional challenges.

There's no reason a single parent shouldn't be able to own a business. Or that anyone has to be 100 percent debt-free to pursue their dreams. Yet this is the world we have to navigate. Instead of calling it for what it is, the few entrepreneurs who become successful pat themselves on the back and wag their fingers at the less fortunate. They position themselves as experts and coaches, teach masterclasses on confidence, and leave out the role privilege plays in their success.

Experts conveniently gloss over the trauma Black women face every day and that still shows up even when we work for ourselves. Every time I hear about a Black woman's experience in the workplace, it validates why I've made the decisions I have. I wanted to re-enlist in the military for financial stability. If I stayed in that environment though, I probably wouldn't be alive today. The same at my first "real" job in California. I felt so much guilt about leaving after less than a year, but my mind and body wouldn't rest until I did. It's terrifying that the decision to stay at or leave a job, is a matter of life or death for Black women. I'm proud that we're starting to choose life. I'm also discouraged when the rest of society looks on nonchalantly, even as we tell them their blueprint to success doesn't work for us. I think of my younger self, who spent years chasing the "golden ticket," the one dream opportunity that would change my life the way it happens in TV shows and movies. Now with a decade of work experience and no golden ticket in sight, I grapple with the truth that it may not exist.

The path forward

I talked to Zanade, founder of the Black Women's Business Collective, about what entrepreneurship looks like for Black women moving forward.[1] Zanade launched the organization after the pandemic's onset to share financial resources with Black women business owners when traditional funding proved to be scarce.

"I felt the need to push for Black women's businesses, instead of using my expertise for everyone outside of our community," she told me.

With more than 15 years of experience in public relations, entertainment, and communications, she tapped into her network to get the organization up and running. While she anticipated pushback because of her specific focus on Black women, most of her peers were on board with her vision and connected her with the right people to start distributing funds.

Her mention of potential pushback moved us into another topic, which is how Black women can make business moves in a system not designed for us to win. Because we're less likely than our white peers to qualify for business loans or secure investments through venture capital funding, how do we bring our dreams to existence? Zanade believes Black women can achieve entrepreneurial success, but only when we play the game differently.

"For all the talk about equity, we're not playing the same game," she said. "I can win, but I have to go about it in a different way."

Rather than focus on traditional strategies to grow a business, she suggests thinking out of the box. A gesture she's made in the past is striking up conversation with people at big-name companies who don't *seem* important to the average person, like an intern or executive assistant. Once she builds a rapport, it allows her to learn about the company from an insider perspective and how she can be an asset. Other ideas include sending cold emails, or reaching out to second-degree connections on LinkedIn and asking for a warm introduction. She said, "I've never gone wrong with a warm intro because it feels easier when someone else connects you."

If you're not having luck with grant applications or other conventional funding, consider crowdfunding platforms like Kickstarter or GoFundMe. These platforms allow you to set up campaigns for specific projects and milestones. Before you take this route, make sure you've connected with your network organically. The more familiar your community is with your work, the better chance you have at reaching your target goal.

Spend time gaining hands-on experience in your area of expertise. This isn't as glamorous as the fancy acronyms on your LinkedIn page, but it positions you as someone your clients can trust. Your target audience cares more about your ability to address their pain points than how many followers you have on TikTok. Create polls or short surveys to find out what they're having trouble with and how you can help. Send thank you cards to current and past clients to let them know you appreciate their business. These small touches help you stand out. Focus on providing the best client experience and the rest will come.

Rather than set our sights on getting a seat at the table, Zanade and I agree that Black women are well equipped to create our own. She said, "In the thick of it, when no one sees the vision, you have to believe in it. That's the risk you take."

Here are some final gems to take with you as you build a table on your terms.

Quality > quantity

Companies, brands, and influencers alike share huge numbers to prove credibility, whether it's a million views on their Youtube channel or 100,000 Instagram followers. While the big sexy numbers seem meaningful, what benefit do they really bring as a business owner? Zanade made a poignant statement that if you have 30,000 followers who never invest in your products or services, it's not much to brag about.

"I coach Black women who own businesses and the first thing they say is, 'I want more followers,'" she told me. "If you don't have a plan to convert those 30,000 followers into customers, what's the point?"

"A lot of us are letting social media use us when we spend massive amounts of time online and get caught up in nonsense. If you're a business owner, you need to talk about what made you start your business."

I've watched my peers set goals to gain 100 followers per month, when they don't engage with the hundreds of followers they have. Meanwhile, I make a point to respond to most comments I get on social media. You don't have to respond to every comment, but genuine engagement with your audience is important. If you want to connect visually, make a short video with a shout out to regular supporters. Offer a gift card give-away to newsletter subscribers a few times throughout the year. When people comment on your blog, thank them for reading your content. You'd be surprised how many bloggers don't do this! As a small business, relationships are everything. Maybe you "only" have 100 followers. If those 100 followers are loyal and tell all their friends about what you do, you'll be in business for the long haul.

Make room for life outside of business

I've been called a workaholic more times in my life than I care to admit. While I often deny it, it's hard to when I spend free time doing research on entrepreneurship and thinking of new ways to reach my target audience. As ambitious as I am, there comes a time when I desperately need to turn my brain off of business mode. It's exciting to see my business grow and find new opportunities, but I have to ask myself what it means if I'm too consumed with work to actually enjoy it?

For Black women, we make so many sacrifices to get ahead in life. We work multiple jobs, enroll in 20 credit hours to complete our degrees, and attend every networking event to get ourselves in front of big industry names. While we excel professionally, we do so at the expense of our own personal fulfillment. Whether we want to believe it or not, the "grind 24/7" mentality can do more harm than good.

We hustle to move up the ladder in the workplace, then turn around and do the same as we build our own businesses. All the while not realizing that we're defeating the purpose of why we decided to work for ourselves in the first place: To reach freedom. Let's challenge ourselves to enjoy life outside of making money. Strike up a conversation with someone without looking at it as a potential business opportunity. Pick up a hobby and don't try to monetize it. We're worth more than our labor regardless of what the world expects from us. I want to see Black women fully embrace and enjoy life without the burdens of capitalism. It's time we find peace and indulge in the fruits of our labor unapologetically.

Zanade put it this way: "You can have everything, just not at the same time. There are things like peace which you can't buy. You have to figure out what to do in your life to get that."

She completed multiple degrees as a single mother of two daughters and focused on doing whatever it took to provide for them with limited resources. Once she gained financial stability, she began to question whether she wanted her life to be all about the hustle.

"I asked myself, 'Do I want to be a hustling ass woman with no relationship and no time for her kids?' The answer was no. My goal was to build generational wealth and I probably could do it alone, but it could happen a little faster with a partner. Which is around the time I met my now-husband."

She's now been with her husband for more than 10 years and is happy to have someone in her life to build a legacy with. Let me be clear. I'm not telling you to settle down with a spouse and kids if that's not what you want. I'm single with no ki and I plan to keep it that way for the time being. How encourage you to explore the "silly" goals that might not move your business forward but still bring you joy. Spend more time with friends and family. Adopt a pet or try your hand at growing a garden. These choices might not directly tie into your business mission, but they give you room to experience life outside of the grind.

Keep your standards high

Every time I lower my standards, whether for a job, friendship, or romantic relationship, I regret it. No matter how many times I tell myself to "just be grateful," I'm not happy. Before long, I cut ties because the weight of staying in a situation that doesn't align with my standards is too heavy to bear. I'm learning to take pride in my standards. Rather than settle for what's in front of me, I put the responsibility on others to raise themselves to my standards or keep it moving. If I hold myself to a high standard, there's no reason I should accept less from anyone else.

What you want for yourself and your business might not seem realistic to people around you. Maybe your goal is to run a business that brings in a million dollars in revenue annually. Or you want to bring in enough passive income so you can take three months of vacation every year. These goals are attainable. They also require some discipline. Does most of your time and energy go into relationships that don't add value to your life? Find ways to scale back. Practice saying no to projects that don't align with your brand. Leave those group chats that focus y gossip than building your craft. Set limits on :olling, and block off times in your schedule respond to emails or texts immediately. u time to sharpen your skills, and get clear on and how to make it happen. You probably on dollars in revenue tomorrow, but you'll be moving in the right direction. Less time on social media means more time to read a book or listen to a podcast by someone who's achieved the milestones you want to reach. Leaving that drama-filled group chat gives you space to seek out a new group to cheer you on and keep you accountable. It won't be easy, but advancing to the next level in your business rarely is. Stay firm, keep your standards high, and trust the stars will align to bring you what you want.

BLACK WOMEN ARE NOT SET up to win in the workplace. When we do, it's often because we've managed to dodge the bullets of corporate America. Still, Black women succeeding in traditional industries is the exception, not the rule. I hope systems change in the future to better support us, but that change won't happen overnight. In the meantime, I want Black women to use entrepreneurship as a tool to take back the power stolen by the toxic infrastructure of employment.

Years ago, I followed an entertainment blogger's website with a tagline that simply read: "I'm not for everybody." This phrase applies perfectly to Black women as we move through life. It's lonely to step outside of what society deems acceptable, but there's beauty in it. When you embrace your unique qualities, you can confidently walk through the doors that start to open for you. Your direct, no-nonsense approach might not help you climb the corporate ladder, but it can help you negotiate a contract that pays your bills for the year. Your passion for social justice may be too radical for a 9-to-5, but it can connect you with like-minded entrepreneurs who support you in your fight to make meaningful change.

For every person who thinks you're too much, there others who recognize how powerful you are. We don't h settle for scraps because companies neglect to inve careers. We are smart, innovative, bold, and dynamic. When we understand we're not for everybody, we give ourselves space to define success on our own terms. And when we define success on our own terms, we release ourselves from the chains of working twice as hard.

ACKNOWLEDGMENTS

Thanks to God and every other divine being for giving me the strength to get this book out into the world. Writing my first book post-divorce, during a pandemic, public attention around racial injustice, and historic political uncertainty is one of the hardest things I've ever done. The fact that I put together words during this time is truly a miracle.

Thank you to my therapist, who gave me the space and support I needed to find myself. I'm forever grateful for your patience, kindness, and words of encouragement.

To Kristin, thank you for being my biggest cheerleader during this process. From your generous offer to edit my hot mess of a first draft to your "just because" gifts, I cherish our connection as writers and friends.

Thank you to my beta readers (Aitza, Crystal Marie, and Taylor) for your time and feedback. Your thoughtful comments warmed my heart!

Much gratitude to everyone who assisted in editing drafts of my work, including Barbra, Kathryn, and Jackie. Each round of edits moved me one step closer to a book I'm deeply proud of.

I appreciate every woman who took the time to share their

stories with me. It was so validating to speak with other Black women and learn more about their experiences.

To my book cover designer Chavon, I can't say enough how much I enjoyed working with you to visualize my idea. Your positive energy and attention to detail is unmatched.

Thank you to the online community that shares, retweets, and sends thoughtful messages about my work. Your support means the world.

And finally, to the Black woman working twice as hard. I hope this book offers you comfort and validation that you're good enough just the way you are.

NOTES

1. Sweet dream...or a nonprofit nightmare

1. Claude Steele and Joshua Aronson, "Stereotype Threat and the Intellectual Test Performance of African Americans," *Journal of Personality and Social Psychology* 69, no. 5, (November 1995): 797-811, https://doi.org/10.1037/0022-3514.69.5.797
2. "2019 American Express State of Women-Owned Businesses Report," *American Express*, September 23, 2019, https://s1.q4cdn.com/692158879/files/doc_library/file/2019-state-of-women-owned-businesses-report.pdf

2. The leap (or push?) from a 9-to-5

1. Jocelyn Frye, "Racism and Sexism Combine to Shortchange Working Black Women," *Center for American Progress*, August 22, 2019, https://www.americanprogress.org/issues/women/news/2019/08/22/473775/racism-sexism-combine-shortchange-working-black-women/
2. "Employed Persons by Occupation, Race, Hispanic or Latino Ethnicity, and Sex," U.S. Bureau of Labor Statistics, last modified January 22, 2021, https://www.bls.gov/cps/cpsaat10.htm
3. Joan C. Williams and Marina Multhaup, "For Women and Minorities to Get Ahead, Managers Must Assign Work Fairly," *Harvard Business Review*, March 5, 2018, https://hbr.org/2018/03/for-women-and-minorities-to-get-ahead-managers-must-assign-work-fairly
4. Madeline E. Heilman and Julie J. Chen, "Same Behavior, Different Consequences: Reactions to Men's and Women's Altruistic Citizenship Behavior," *Journal of Applied Psychology*, 90, no. 3, (May 2005): 431–441, https://psycnet.apa.org/doi/10.1037/0021-9010.90.3.431
5. Ashleigh Shelby Rosette and Robert W. Livingston, "Failure is Not an Option for Black Women: Effects of Organizational Performance on Leaders with Single versus Dual-Subordinate Identities," *Journal of Experimental Social Psychology*, 48, no. 5, (September 2012): 1162-1167, https://doi.org/10.1016/j.jesp.2012.05.002
6. Jack Guy, "Black Women with Natural Hairstyles are Less Likely to Get Job Interviews," *CNN Business*, August 12, 2020, https://www.cnn.com/2020/08/12/business/black-women-hairstyles-interview-scli-intl-scn/index.html

7. Pamela Avila, "California Just Became the First State to Ban Discrimination Against Natural Hair," *Los Angeles Magazine*, July 3, 2019, https://www.lamag.com/citythinkblog/crown-act-signed-natural-hair/
8. Sarah O'Brien, "Here's How the Wage Gap Affects Black Women," *CNBC*, August 22, 2019, https://www.cnbc.com/2019/08/22/heres-how-the-gender-wage-gap-affects-this-minority-group.html
9. "Raise Anatomy: How to Ask for a Raise and Get It," *Payscale*, June 5, 2018, https://www.payscale.com/data/how-to-ask-for-a-raise
10. "Workplace Stress on the Rise With 83% of Americans Frazzled by Something at Work," *Globe Newswire*, April 9, 2013, https://www.globe-newswire.com/news-release/2013/04/09/536945/10027728/en/Workplace-Stress-on-the-Rise-With-83-of-Americans-Frazzled-by-Something-at-Work.html
11. Joel Goh, Jeffrey Pfeffer, and Stefanos Zenios, "The Relationship Between Workplace Stressors and Mortality and Health Costs in the United States," *Management Science*, 62, no. 2, (March 13, 2015): 608-628, https://doi.org/10.1287/mnsc.2014.2115
12. Maura Cheeks, "The Psychic Stress of Being the Only Black Woman at Work," *Lenny Letter*, January 16, 2018, https://www.lennyletter.com/story/the-stress-of-being-the-only-black-woman-at-work
13. Kassandra in discussion with the author, April 22, 2020.
14. Sherrhonda R. Gibbs, "The Bitter Truth: A Comparative Analysis of Black Male and Black Female Entrepreneurs," Journal of Developmental Entrepreneurship, 19, no. 1, (April 2014): 1450006, https://doi.org/10.1142/S108494671450006X

3. Healing from work wounds

1. Joy Harden Bradford, Ph.D. and Samara Stone, LCSW-C, "Session 87: Entrepreneurship & Mental Health," *Therapy for Black Girls*, December 12, 2018, https://therapyforblackgirls.com/2020/01/09/session-87-entrepreneurship-mental-health/

4. The cost to be a boss

1. Christian E. Weller, "African Americans Face Systematic Obstacles to Getting Good Jobs," *Center For American Progress*, December 5, 2019, https://www.americanprogress.org/issues/economy/reports/2019/12/05/478150/african-americans-face-systematic-obstacles-getting-good-jobs/
2. Edna Bonhomme, "Debt is Holding Black Americans Hostage," *The Nation*, November 7, 2019, https://www.thenation.com/article/archive/debt-is-holding-black-americans-hostage/

3. "From Cradle to Cane: The Cost of Being a Female Consumer," The New York City Department of Consumer Affairs, December 18, 2015, https://www1.nyc.gov/assets/dca/downloads/pdf/partners/Study-of-Gender-Pricing-in-NYC.pdf
4. Lynn Parramore, "Like Abusive Policing, Denial of Access to Mortgage Credit for Black Americans is a Growing Crisis," *Institute for New Economic Thinking*, October 31, 2016, https://www.ineteconomics.org/perspectives/blog/like-abusive-policing-denial-of-access-to-mortgage-credit-for-black-americans-is-growing-crisis
5. Robert Bartlett, Adair Morse, Richard Stanton, and Nancy Wallace, "Consumer-Lending Discrimination in the FinTech Era," University of California, Berkeley, November 2019, http://faculty.haas.berkeley.edu/morse/research/papers/discrim.pdf

5. I just want to be successful

1. Nia (not her real name) in discussion with the author, May 6, 2020.
2. Megan Cerullo, "Up to 90% of Minority and Women Owners Shut out of Paycheck Protection Program, Experts Fear," *CBS News*, April 22, 2020, https://www.cbsnews.com/news/women-minority-business-owners-paycheck-protection-program-loans/
3. "Diversity in U.S. Startups," RateMyInvestor, 2019, https://ratemyinvestor.com/pdfjs/full?file=%2FDiversityVCReport_Final.pdf
4. Kathryn Finney, "The State of Black Women Founders: PROJECTDIANE 2018," *Medium*, June 13, 2018, https://medium.com/@Kathryn-Finney/the-state-of-black-women-founders-projectdiane-2018-a93f8-fa8bfa1
5. Chandra Steele, "Give Your Money to Black Women," *PCMag*, March 10, 2020, https://medium.com/pcmag-access/give-your-money-to-black-women-b5411f4073de
6. Sarah Blakeslee, "The CRAAP Test," *LOEX Quarterly*, 31, no. 3, article 4, October 2004, https://commons.emich.edu/loexquarterly/vol31/iss3/4

6. Same shit, different (work) day

1. Tiffany Hsu and Sandra E. Garcia, "A Rush to Use Black Art Leaves the Artists Feeling Used," *The New York Times*, July 20, 2020, https://www.nytimes.com/2020/07/20/business/media/black-creatives-protests.html
2. Kamala Harris, "2020 Vice Presidential Debate," October 7, 2020, University of Utah, Salt Lake City, Utah.
3. Maiysha Kai, "The Significance of 'I'm Speaking,'" *The Root*, October 8, 2020, https://theglowup.theroot.com/the-significance-of-im-speaking-1845313016

7. Putting on a brave face

1. Inger E. Burnett-Zeigler, "The Strong and Stressed Black Woman," *The New York Times*, April 25, 2018, https://www.nytimes.com/2018/04/25/opinion/strong-stressed-black-woman.html
2. "COVID-19 Mortality Overview," Centers for Disease Control and Prevention, last reviewed January 27, 2021, https://www.cdc.gov/nchs/covid19/mortality-overview.htm
3. "Demographics of the U.S. Military," Council on Foreign Relations, last updated July 13, 2020, https://www.cfr.org/backgrounder/demographics-us-military
4. Jorge Guadardo (@jorge_guadardo), "Black women will save the United States," Twitter, August 17, 2020, https://twitter.com/jorge_guajardo/status/1295556454473256961?lang=en
5. @FreshwithDepth, "Yall [sic] don't pay us equally. Don't promote us within your organizations. Don't credit us for our ideas or style or impact. Don't allow us the spaces or outlets," Twitter, August 17, 2020, https://twitter.com/FreshWithDepth/status/1295566645667205121

8. Back in bed with the enemy

1. "Survival of Private Sector Establishments by Opening Year," U.S. Bureau of Labor Statistics, accessed February 22, 2021, https://www.bls.gov/bdm/us_age_naics_00_table7.txt
2. Tomi in discussion with the author, September 22, 2020.
3. Sarah in email to the author, February 24, 2021.

9. Does a golden ticket exist?

1. Zanade in discussion with the author, November 10, 2020.

ABOUT THE AUTHOR

Quinisha Jackson-Wright is a U.S. Navy veteran, freelance journalist, and blogger with bylines in The New York Times, Wired, Business Insider, and The Muse. She lives and works in California.

twitter.com/KWright0702
instagram.com/kwright0702
linkedin.com/in/quinisha-jackson-wright